Taekwondo

A Comprehensive Guide to Tae Kwon Do Techniques, Basics, and Tenets for Beginners Wanting to Master This Martial Art

Contents

INTRODUCTION 1

CHAPTER 1: A BRIEF HISTORY OF TAEKWONDO 3

    ANCIENT HISTORY 4

    JAPANESE OCCUPATION 5

    MODERN TAEKWONDO 6

    THE TAEKWONDO ASSOCIATIONS 7

    TAEKWONDO IN AMERICA 8

CHAPTER 2: THE ORIGINAL MASTERS OF TAEKWONDO 11

CHAPTER 3: GRADING AND THE TAEKWONDO BELT SYSTEM 15

    WHAT TO EXPECT ON GRADING DAY 16

    WHO ARE THE EXAMINERS? 17

    GRADING RESULTS 17

    TIME REQUIREMENTS AND GRADES 18

    WHAT A GRADING TEST ENTAILS 19

CHAPTER 4: FUNDAMENTAL MOVEMENTS IN TAEKWONDO 21

    THE STANCES 22

    THE PRINCIPLES PROPER TAEKWONDO STANCE 22

    BLOCKS 29

    ATTACKS 32

OTHER COMMON ATTACK MOVES 37

CHAPTER 5: MEDITATION AND TAEKWONDO 39

BREATH AND FOCUS 40

MASTERING MEDITATION - TIPS TO BEGIN 41

UNDERSTANDING THE CONNECTION BETWEEN MARTIAL ARTS AND
MEDITATION... 43

MINDFULNESS AND TAEKWONDO 44

CHAPTER 6: THE 24 ESSENTIAL PATTERNS IN TAEKWONDO 47

WHY ARE THERE 24 ESSENTIAL PATTERNS? 48

THE 24 ESSENTIAL PATTERNS IN TAEKWONDO 49

IMPORTANT TIPS TO NOTE WHEN PERFORMING TAEKWONDO
PATTERNS... 55

CHAPTER 7: THE FIVE TENETS OF TAEKWONDO 56

ANALYZING THE TENETS... 58

CHAPTER 8: TAEKWONDO HAND TECHNIQUES 64

PUNCHES ARE A SECRET WEAPON... 65

HOW TO THROW A GOOD PUNCH IN TAEKWONDO............................. 65

TAEKWONDO HAND TECHNIQUES.. 67

DIFFERENCES IN HAND TECHNIQUE RULES BETWEEN TAEKWONDO
ORGANIZATIONS... 74

TIPS FOR IMPROVING YOUR HAND TECHNIQUES IN TAEKWONDO 75

EXERCISES TO IMPROVE YOUR HAND TECHNIQUES........................... 76

CHAPTER 9: TAEKWONDO FOOT TECHNIQUES...........................77

TIPS FOR IMPROVING YOUR KICKS IN TAEKWONDO 86

STRETCHING EXERCISES AND TAEKWONDO 88

OTHER EXERCISES TO INCREASE THE SPEED AND POWER OF YOUR
KICKS... 90

TIPS FOR EFFECTIVE KICK PRACTICE IN TAEKWONDO...................... 91

CHAPTER 10: SELF-DEFENSE IN TAEKWONDO 93

IMPORTANCE OF TAEKWONDO SELF-DEFENSE................................. 94

SELF-DEFENSE TECHNIQUES 95

YOU ONLY NEED THE BASICS.. 95

Basic Taekwondo Moves That Are Useful for Self-Defense............ 96

Self-Defense Techniques in Different Situations................................ 99

Linear and Circular Taekwondo Self-Defense Techniques 101

CHAPTER 11: THE ART OF BLOCKING IN TAEKWONDO 102

Basic Principles of Blocking 103

How Blocks Are Classified in Taekwondo 104

Classification of Blocks Based on the Blocking Level 104

Other Ways Blocks Are Classified.. 106

Common Blocks in Taekwondo 107

Tips for Practicing Your Taekwondo Blocks................................. 110

CHAPTER 12: STRETCHES AND DRILLS 111

Importance of Stretching 112

Different Kinds of Stretches 114

Understanding Taekwondo Drills... 117

Additional Things to Note... 118

CHAPTER 13: THE TAEKWONDO HABIT: TRAINING, DISCIPLINE, AND MINDSET 121

What Can One Learn from Taekwondo?.. 122

CONCLUSION...128

HERE'S ANOTHER BOOK BY CLINT SHARP THAT YOU MIGHT LIKE 130

REFERENCES 131

Introduction

Like any other sport, getting started with Taekwondo can be daunting for beginners. While it bears some similarities to other martial arts forms, it is remarkably different in various ways, which is why you need to learn the basics to be able to lay a solid foundation for your journey.

Taekwondo, as a combat sport, has a history that spans several centuries. The early precursors of the sport date back over 2000 years. Translated as "the ways of hands and feet," the sport bears semblance to many ancient martial arts that were eventually unified during the 1940s and 1950s.

Taekwondo is a combative contact sport, but it's not an unruly free-for-all. There are rules, as well as specific techniques that the person has to adhere to. More than its physicality, there are unique principles and tenets that must be learned. Taekwondo also teaches discipline with an emphasis on developing the mind just as much as the body.

Taekwondo is for everyone and is a great way to work out, build your strength, develop excellent leadership skills, and improve yourself overall. Do you want to get started with Taekwondo and enjoy all of its benefits? Come along as we go through the basics, tenets, and techniques of this ancient martial art.

Chapter 1: A Brief History of Taekwondo

Taekwondo is a Korean Martial Art characterized by quick and powerful leg kicks. The name of the art translates to "the way of the foot and fist." Today, Taekwondo is one of the most well-known forms of martial arts and the easiest styles to learn for anyone of any age worldwide.

Although the original forms of martial arts from which Taekwondo takes its roots go way back, it has a very short history in its current form. It is young compared to other forms of Asian martial arts, like Karate.

The development of Taekwondo as we know it today began in the 1940s. The art came about through the work of various martial artists. It was born from a combination of older art forms like Chinese martial arts and Korean martial arts, such as Taekkyeon, which is focused on dynamic footwork and striking; Subak, the martial art predecessor of Taekkyeon; and Gwonbeop, which is the Korean version of the Chinese martial arts.

Ancient History

As mentioned earlier, even though Taekwondo is relatively young, it draws its root from ancient Korean martial art forms. Therefore, it is impossible to talk about the history of Taekwondo without making a brief reference to how these older martial art forms came about.

According to ancient Korean mythology, the Korean Nation was founded in 2333 B.C. by the Tangun or Dangun (god-kings). However, there are no records of any martial arts during this period. The first mention of martial arts is linked to the Three Kingdoms era. Our Taekwondo history begins with the establishment of these three kingdoms: Silla, Goguryeo, and Baekje, in 57 B.C., 37 B.C., and 18 B.C., respectively.

During the three kingdoms era, the Silla Kingdom, which was the smallest of these three, requested help from the Baekje to defend itself from the Goguryeo and pirates that terrorized it. The Baekje kingdom had a basic style of martial arts, which they taught the Silla soldiers to help them defend their kingdom.

Chin Heung, Silla's 24th king, elevated this martial art's popularity by incorporating it into fundamental military training programs. He formed a group of young fighters skilled in martial arts. Hwa Rang Do was their chosen name; it translates into "Flowering Youth."

The Subak, the martial art practiced by this group of soldiers, was one of the early predecessors of Taekwondo. They also learned to command weaponry such as swords, bows, and spears in addition to physical combat. Subak practice also included lectures in ethical rules that paralleled Buddhist monks' teachings. These included selflessness and dedication to serving the kingdom and its people and leading an exemplary lifestyle. These principles are similar to many of the tenets of Taekwondo that are still taught today.

The Hwa Rang Do troops were highly successful in military conquests, and through their help, the Kingdom of Silla defeated its enemies. This victory also led to the unification of the three separate kingdoms into a single kingdom in the Korean Peninsula.

In 936 A.D., Wang Kon formed the Koryo Kingdom, and the Subak (hand combat) was the adopted style of martial arts. In addition to being used for military combat, it was also practiced for self-defense and as a form of exercise.

As the art quickly became a favorite pastime of the people, men who practiced the art of Subak were widely respected. It was popular among citizens of the Koryo Dynasty, very much the same way American Football is well-known in the United States today.

During this time, Subak became more than just military combat training and was taught to commoners, boosting its popularity.

During the 1300s, the Subak martial arts style evolved into the Taekkyeon, a form of art that emphasized kicking. The history of the name "Tae-kwon-do" has also been linked to Taekkyeon.

During the Joseon Dynasty (Yi Dynasty), which lasted from 1392 to 1910, the country's military changed its philosophical ideals from Buddhism to Confucianism. An implication of this was that the once-popular martial arts of Subak and Teakkyeon became unpopular among the elites and the ruling class; they were only practiced by commoners.

Japanese Occupation

The Japanese invaded Korea in 1909 and occupied the country until World War II ended in 1945. During this period, all elements of Korean culture were suppressed, and the Japanese government banned all things connected to Korean heritage and art forms, including Teakkyeon and Subak.

Japanese and Chinese martial arts were taught instead of the traditional Korean martial arts. As a result of this suppression, many Taekkyeon and Subak masters had to go into hiding or escape to other countries to continue teaching and practicing their art.

Modern Taekwondo

The era of the modern Taekwondo began after World War II, which signaled the freedom of the Korean Peninsula. Once again, the Koreans were now free to practice their traditional martial arts.

From 1945, several new martial arts schools were opened in Seoul, South Korea, to teach the arts of Subak and Taekkyeon. These schools all claimed to teach "genuine" or "traditional" Korean martial arts methods. Not only were these arts diverse, but they also included elements of what they learned during the Japanese occupation, including Kung Fu and Karate techniques.

By the 1960s, nine notable martial arts schools (also known as Kwans), each practicing a slightly different style, existed. But they all bore some similarities to the ancient arts of Subak and Taekkyeon.

Despite being distinct in their techniques and incorporating characteristics of foreign martial arts, the many kinds of martial arts practiced in the Kwans are sometimes lumped together as "Traditional Taekwondo." Around this period, the South Korean military chose to elect traditional Taekkyeon as the official unarmed combat martial art, greatly increasing its popularity. In 1952 during a Taekkyeon demonstration by the military, South Korea's President, Syngman Rhee, was so impressed that he made it mandatory for all of the country's soldiers to be trained in the art. General Choi Hung-hi, a captain at the time, was saddled with the responsibility of formulating standardized training that would return the ancient arts of Subak and Taekkyeon to their roots. This involved uniting the nine different Kwans and stripping their various techniques of all Kung Fu and Karate influence.

By 1955, the masters of all the different Kwans had collaborated to form a single Korean martial arts technique. Tae Soo Do was the original name of the newly established style - from the Korean word *Tae*, to "stomp or trample;" *Soo*, as in "hand"; and *Do*, for "way" or "discipline."

General Choi Hong Hi later suggested that the word "Soo" be replaced with Kwon, meaning "fist." Hence, the name Tae Kwon Do was born." This unified name and newly established techniques were adopted by the various Kwans that taught the art.

The Taekwondo Associations

A few years later, in September of 1961, the Korean Taekwondo Association was officially formed as part of the efforts to further standardize the activities of the various Kwans. The KTA became the Taekwondo governing body for the entire country and was headed by none other than General Choi.

Under the General's administration, the art of Taekwondo received some major boosts. Masters of the art were sent to a number of locations worldwide in order to spread proper teachings of Taekwondo, in addition to establishing an esteemed representation of the country. He also laid the groundwork for the creation of an international body called the International Taekwondo Federation, which would have its headquarters in South Korea.

As head of the KTA, General Choi played an important role in the development and popularity of the art. However, his ambitious efforts to grow Taekwondo eventually brought him into disfavor with the people and government of Korea. He sent a delegation of Taekwondo instructors to North Korea for a diplomatic mission in 1966. This did not bode well with the South Korean government since the countries were at war with each other; General Choi was then relieved of his position.

Enraged, General Choi left the country and moved to Toronto, Canada. From there, he created the International Taekwondo Federation and dissociated himself from the KTA in 1972. The International Taekwondo Federation is focused more on the Traditional Taekwondo style that was created and refined by General Choi.

The South Korean government established a new national academy to teach Taekwondo a year after the ITF was formed. This academy was called the Kukkiwon. The World Taekwondo Federation was also created at this time. The purpose of the WTF was to promote Taekwondo at international levels.

The style and rules of Taekwondo adopted by the WTF are known as the Kukkiwon style or WTF style. It is also the same as the Olympic style or sports style. WTF's efforts ensured the recognition of Taekwondo as an international sport. Currently, Taekwondo is one of only two Asian martial arts (including Judo) that compete at the Olympics. In 2010, it was also recognized as a sport at the Commonwealth Games.

Taekwondo in America

In 1962, Jhoon Goo Rhee established the first Taekwondo school in America, in Washington DC. Rhee is often reputed as the Father of American Taekwondo, but prior to his arrival, there were other masters of the sport in the country. Taekwondo masters first arrived in the United States from Korea to teach the art in the 1960s. They came as representatives of the KTA at the time. In 1963, a Taekwondo demonstration was conducted in the United States and was favorably welcomed, leading to the formation of the United States Taekwondo Federation under the supervision of the Amateur Athletic Union and the United States Taekwondo Union. The WTF acknowledged the United States Taekwondo Union as the regulatory organization for tournaments in the United States in 1984. The United States Olympic Committee took over the Union in 2004 due to an internal problem, and the sport was renamed USA Taekwondo the following year. Haeng Un Lee founded the American Taekwondo Association in 1969 after going to meet General Choi in 1968 to learn traditional Taekwondo. The organization's headquarters are in Little Rock, Arkansas, and it boasts over 350,000 members who participate in the sport. The Songaham style of Taekwondo is the one used by the ATA (Pine Tree and Rock style). In this approach, s tudents are referred to as a pine tree that grows from a weak little sapling to a big, magnificent tree with rock-solid roots. The ATA has highly rigorous requirements, and schools that are members are obligated to implement the association's business model. The ATA is run like a business, with a CEO (who is required to have a 9th-degree black belt) and a board of decision-makers.WTF and Olympic History

The World Taekwondo Federation has been linked with different Taekwondo schools in over 160 countries since 1973. The organization's headquarters are located in Kukkiwon, Seoul, South Korea. Since 1980, the International Olympic Committee (IOC) has recognized the organization as the sport's official governing body. According to the organization's official website, there are currently more than 5 million WTF certified black belt holders. Taekwondo made its Olympic debut as a demonstration sport in 1988 and then again in 1992. At the 2000 Olympics in Sydney, Australia, it was formally acknowledged as an Olympic sport.

WTF practices and training tend to lean more towards the sports-like form of Taekwondo than ITF styles, which are more centered on traditional Taekwondo. Many master teachers, however, maintain that certain traditional Taekwondo aspects are still present in WTF training programs. The World Taekwondo Federation sanctioned and promoted international, national, regional, and local Taekwondo tournaments. The WTF also promotes the sport in local communities through academic institutions (also known as Dojangs) that teach martial arts to adults and children to better their fitness and physical health. Its method is comparable to that of the ancient Hwa Rang Do technique, which taught the Subak art to commoners.

Chapter 2: The Original Masters of Taekwondo

The pioneer masters of taekwondo are a group of 12 South Korean martial arts instructors who created the Korea Taekwondo Association (KTA) in the 1960s to promote the latest forms of martial art. Many of the men on the list had prominent roles in the International Taekwondo Federation (ITF), but as time went on, the majority of them moved to North America, Australia, and Europe. The title "Original Masters" does not imply that these individuals were the first KTA masters, though. The KTA was founded by nine men who headed their own kwans, a distinct set of individuals than those on the list we'll discuss. But many of them practiced martial arts under different names, such as kong soo do and tae soo do, refusing to use the name taekwondo. Below is a list of the first men to ever adopt that name and actively promote it.

- **Choi Chang Keun**

C K Choi was born in Korea in 1940 and began his martial arts training in the Korean army in 1956. He began teaching taekwondo in Malaysia in 1964 and relocated to Vancouver in 1970. He was promoted to 8th dan in 1981 and 9th dan in 2002 after starting as a 7th dan in 1973. To this day, he is still living in Vancouver.

- Choi Kwang Jo

K J Choi was born in Daegu, Korea, in March 1942, and he began training in the martial arts as a child. Choi met Hong Hi Choi while serving in the South Korean army. He instructed students in taekwondo all over Singapore, Malaysia, Indonesia, and Hong Kong in 1966/67. Injuries experienced during training, however, led him to seek medical care in the United States in 1970. In 1987, he formed the Choi Kwang-Do organization and now resides in Atlanta. He is ranked 9th dan in Choi Kwang-do.

- Han Cha Kyo

Born in Seoul, Korea in 1934, C K Han trained under no less than three masters – Woon Kyu Um, Duk Sung Son, and Tae Hi Nam. In March 1959, he was the first original master to perform taekwondo outside of Korea while traveling to Vietnam and Taiwan. After quitting the South Korean army in 1971, he immigrated to the United States and resided in Chicago. In 1980, he founded the Universal Taekwondo Foundation and continued to teach until he died in 1996.

- Kim Jong Chan

Born in 1937, J C Kim taught taekwondo in the 1960s in Malaysia. In 1979, while ranked 7th dan, he traveled to Argentina to show and teach taekwondo. Chan was listed as the President of the World Tukido Council in a letter he wrote, which was later published in the Black Belt magazine in July 1985. Today, he lives in Vancouver, Canada.

- Kim Kwang II

K I Kim made a significant contribution to introducing taekwondo in West Germany and, until 1971, he was the ITF head instructor in West Germany. In 1975, he was elevated to 6th dan, and in 1976, he promoted Rolf Becking, the leader of the ITF Germany Technical Committee, to 2nd dan. He operated his own restaurant in Stuttgart from 1974 to 1977 and finished his Brewmeister training before opening.

• Kong Young II

Y I Kong was born in Korea in 1943 and began training in Shotgun Karate in 1952. He served in the South Korean army from 1963 to 1967, rising to the rank of Sergeant. Throughout his time and after leaving the army, he took part in demonstrations worldwide and emigrated to the USA around 1968. In 1968, he and his brother, Young Bo Kong, formed the Young Brothers Taekwondo Associates, and in 1997, H H Choi advanced him to 9th dan in Poland. He is currently residing in Las Vegas.

• Park Jong Soo

Born in Chung-Nam, South Korea, in 1947, J S Park trained under H H Choi. He traveled to West Germany in 1965 to take over as coach of the German Taekwondo Association. He relocated to the Netherlands in 1966, where he established the association's Dutch division. He moved to Canada in 1968 and still resides there now, holding the level of 9th dan.

• Park Jung Tae

H T Park was born in Korea in 1943/44 (it's unclear which year) and learned boxing as a kid before moving on to judo and taekwondo. He was head of military taekwondo training from 1965 to 1967 in Vietnam before moving to Canada in 1970. In 1984, he was ranked 8th dan in the ITF but, due to political issues, he departed the ITF in 1989. He formed the Global Taekwondo Federation in 1990 and resided in Mississauga until 2002, where he died.

• Park Sun Jae

S JPark, one of the founders of taekwondo, visited Croatia in 1964 to deliver lectures on the martial art. He presented it in Italy in 1968 and was graded 5th dan at the time, rising to 7th dan in 1975. In 1976, during the foundation's inaugural meeting, he was chosen Vice-President of the European Taekwondo Union. He joined the WTF World Cup championship arbitration board in 2002 and was named Acting President of the WTF in 2004, following the resignation of Un

Yong Kim. He is still the Vice-President of the World Taekwondo Federation for Italy, and he was elected President of the Italian Taekwondo Federation in 1998.

• Rhee Chong Chul

CC Rhee was born in Korea in 1935 and grew up practicing martial arts, gymnastics, boxing, weightlifting, and basketball. For three years, he served in the Korean Marines as an unarmed combat teacher, instructing the Marine Commandos, Marine Brigade Headquarters, and the Marine 2nd Infantry Division. Rhee was one of the pioneers in spreading taekwondo to Southeast Asia, primarily Singapore and Malaysia, as well as Brunei, Indonesia, and Hong Kong. In about 1965, he founded the Rhee Taekwondo Organization in Australia and still lives in Sydney.

• Rhee Chong Hyup

Born in Korea in 1940, C H Rhee helped introduce Taekwondo to Singapore and Malaysia in the mid-1960s. He moved to Melbourne, Australia, in 1970 and heads up the Melbourne operations of the Rhee Taekwondo Organization.

• Rhee Ki Ha

Born in Seoul, Korea, in 1938, K H Rhee began training at 7 or 8 years of age. He served in the South Korean army, where he met H H Choi and learned taekwondo. In 1964, he began teaching taekwondo to Royal Air Force personnel stationed in Singapore, and in 1967, he relocated to London, England. In 981, he was ranked 8th dan and attained 9th dan in St Petersburg in 1997. He is now renowned as the Father of both Irish and British taekwondo and is currently located in Glasgow.

Chapter 3: Grading and the Taekwondo Belt System

In Taekwondo, the colored belts are referred to as Kup Grades, and they symbolize the rank an individual has attained in the sport. Interestingly, the current grading system was not an original part of the sport; the complex grading system was introduced when Taekwondo made it to the western world.

Originally students merely went from white belt to black belt after years of dedicated practice and training. However, it was discovered that this format would not suit Western practitioners who preferred to have an incentive to continue participating in training. Therefore, the belt grading system was introduced.

In addition to achieving the main solid colors, tags were further introduced to create 9 different belts (stages or gups). Students must work their way up from white to yellow, green, blue, red, and finally, the black belt.

The frequency of grading or promotion depends on how often a student trains. The more lessons you attend and the harder you practice, the more likely you will get your next belt. The grading system includes a test for physical techniques, and students are also required to have the right attitude based on the tenets of martial arts.

Grading is scheduled on a 3-months basis, but students may not grade every time unless they have been practicing consistently and are extremely dedicated. There is a minimum number of lessons that a student must complete before grading for the next stage. There are also specific techniques that must be mastered and a list of translations on which you will be tested. All of these are typically spelled out in a syllabus.

Students typically need 3 to 4 years of rigorous practice to get from white to black belt. However, this duration could be longer or shorter depending on specific circumstances and how hard a student practices.

While instructors assist and guide you with your training, every student's responsibility is to practice and master their grading requirements. Once a student has covered the required number of lessons for grading, the instructor will include them in the pre-grading assessment to determine if they are ready to be graded for the next stage.

What to Expect on Grading Day

Your instructor will inform you of the day and venue of your grading. Students are expected to turn up in a clean and well-ironed uniform with the completed grading form on grading day. At the venue, students line up as if in a regular class. The examiners introduce themselves and give them a breakdown of the order for the day.

Typically, students sit at the back of the hall in their respective grade groups and will be invited forward when it's time for their exam. The exam gauges students based on the standard techniques for each grade, including the basics, routines, sparring, and breaking techniques. Additionally, students will also be tested on Taekwondo theory and translation.

When you are called to do your exam, your name will be announced, and you will be pointed to the starting position for your grading, usually marked with an X on the floor. When your name is called, reply with, "Yes Sir," and run to the spot. Take an attention stance, raise your hands, and mention your name and grade level, e.g., John Doe, 10th Kup, Sir, bow, and take a ready position as you wait for the examiner's instructions to begin.

Who Are the Examiners?

Taekwondo grading examiners usually consist of top instructors. They will observe going through the grading requirements of your grade's syllabus and grade you based on your performance. If you have practiced well, you should be confident you'll perform well and please the examiners.

Grading Results

Grading results are typically announced about a week after a grading exam by your instructor during a normal lesson. New belts or tags and a graded certificate will be assigned to students who have passed. You would also receive a graded certificate. The standard Taekwondo grade results are either pass or fail. If you did not pass, your instructor must explain the reasons and work with you to prepare for your next grading test. If you only narrowly pass, your instructor may require you to take more lessons for an extended period before taking your next grading test.

An A pass may also be assigned for students who pass excellently. But this is rare as it requires the student to have a high mark in every area of grading. In this case, they may be able to take their next grading test as soon as a month of training for it.

Time Requirements and Grades

It takes time to go through all the grades of Taekwondo, and the standard time requirement between each grade gets progressively longer as you go from white to black belt. The blue and the black belts are the two major milestone grades that indicate a substantial step up.

Your Taekwondo syllabus contains details of the requirements for each grade, including the number of hours of lessons you participate in to qualify for a grading test. Note that these times are only considered a minimum. Your instructor may choose to delay your grading based on his assessment of your performance.

- White Belt (10th Kup) – Minimum of 3 months training and 20 lessons

- White Belt, Yellow Tag (9th Kup) - Minimum of 3 months training and 20 lessons

- Yellow Belt (8th Kup) - Minimum of 3 months training and 20 lessons

- Yellow Belt, Green Tag (7th Kup) - Minimum of 3 months training and 30 lessons

- Green Belt (6th Kup) - Minimum of 3 months training and 30 lessons

- Green Belt, Blue Tag (5th Kup) - Minimum of 3 months training and 40 lessons

- Blue Belt (4th Kup) - Minimum of 6 months training and 60 lessons

- Blue Belt, Red Tag (3rd Kup) - Minimum of 6 months training and 70 lessons

- Red Belt (2nd Kup) - Minimum of 6 months training and 70 lessons

- Red Belt, Black Tag (1st Kup) - Minimum of 6 months training and 80 lessons

- Black Belt (1st Dan)

While the black belt is often considered the ultimate, it is, in fact, only the beginning. There are additional Dan grades and other Taekwondo qualifications to attain even as a black belt holder.

What a Grading Test Entails

During your grading, you will be tested on various things. In addition to demonstrating the moves for your grade level, you will also be tested on translations, breaking, and your sparring performance.

Translations

The translations you will be required to learn according to your grade level are included in the syllabus, but the list is only a guide. You may be tested on any translation that the examiner feels you should know for your grade level and lower grades. The translations include the Korean terms used for moves and stances in Taekwondo; hence you should be familiar with them.

Breaking

Demolition grading is not for everyone, and only students over the age of 16 will be required to participate in this as part of their grading. Each grade has a specific set of techniques you must use to break bricks or boards made of wood and tile. Your assessment will be based on your technique, accuracy, power, and ability to break the board.

Before attempting to break, you will demonstrate the technique by slowly touching the target. This way, the examiner can assess your technique and judge if you are doing it correctly and striking the board safely. After this, you have a few attempts to break the board.

Be sure to have practiced the various breaking techniques for your grade before the grading test. Aim at the center of the board and strike through it (not just at it). Confidence is one of the things examiners look for, so take a deep breath and hit the board without hesitation.

Partner Work

While demonstrating some techniques, such as sparring and self-defense, a partner will be required. Usually, the examiners will select a partner who is another student attempting the same grade.

The examiner's assessment of your performance is based on your technique, respect, and control as you work with your partner. You may also be required to work with different partners during a performance, as examiners do this to assess how you respond to different people based on their skill level compared to yours.

At the start of any of these activities, your examiner will give you clear instructions before calling you to attention.

Chapter 4: Fundamental Movements in Taekwondo

There are over 3000 movements, which are the basic elements of Taekwondo, often likened to musical notes. When linked correctly, they produce a harmonious result adding grace and beauty to the sport.

The fundamental movements in Taekwondo involve all parts of the body, performed harmoniously based on the theory of power. Students at all grade levels are expected to practice these movements and gain mastery over each. This way, they can make use of them as needed.

Mastering the fundamental movements is the core of Taekwondo training. These movements are typically a combination of designated positions with specific hand and foot techniques, but other body parts like the head and knees are also involved. In addition to mastering the basic movement, Taekwondo students are expected to know about hand attacking weapons and the vital spots of the opponent's body. A combination of all these movements constitutes a formidable attack or effective defense.

In Taekwondo, each of the basic moves signifies an assault, counterattack, or defense against a specific target region or an action against a real or imagined opponent (or opponents). It's critical to understand how these fundamental motions tie into your overall competency as a learner while studying them. It determines how they will be applied in actual combat.

With constant practice, the Taekwondo movements will become second nature to you. Students must strive to improve the power and balance of their moves and shift stances to block or attack an opponent without losing form.

You will learn to physically use these fundamental motions against actual moving opponents during sparring once you have mastered them in individual training.

The Stances

The stance refers to how you stand and is arguably the most important aspect of learning Taekwondo and any other form of martial arts. The stance is an essential elemental factor on which all your future lessons rest and the reason it must be mastered from the onset.

In Taekwondo, there are numerous stances that students should learn and master. Each stance has an important role in developing the attack and defense and is also essential for developing a student's physical strength.

Taekwondo stances are the foundation on which all the offensive and defensive moves are built. Maintaining the proper stance is vital for performing any kick, punch, or block correctly. Not appreciating the importance of maintaining a good stance will result in loss of balance and power. The appropriate posture also allows you to throw punches and kicks with more accuracy.

The Principles Proper Taekwondo Stance

Each stance in Taekwondo has a specific purpose. For instance, the walking stance gives you a strong base for forward and backward techniques. The sitting stance gives you a solid base to perform lateral strikes improving your forward technique. The L-stance is primarily a fighting stance.

It is extremely important that you master the principles of maintaining the proper posture for each stance from the onset of your Taekwondo training. This will aid you in developing some muscle memory, gradually making each movement smoother and more effortless. As you progress in your training or applied sparring challenges, your movements will become more complicated, and your body will naturally utilize any needed stance that was previously learned.

You only need to understand the principles and familiarize how a correct stance feels, and with time, you will perform them correctly without a need to check. Some principles of a correct stance include:

- **Balance:** Like every other form of martial art, balance is important in Taekwondo. Instructors often stress the importance of balance; without it, there will always be flaws in your stance and consequently in your attack and defense.

- **Relax:** A tense body cannot produce the correct moves, so you must relax your body while in every stance. It gives more fluidity to your moves and helps you quickly react when it's necessary. Later in this book, you will learn about meditation and how it helps calm your mind in Taekwondo.

- **Keep Your Back Straight:** For every stance, your back must be straight and aligned. If your spine isn't aligned as it should be, your base will most likely be off.

- **Tighten Your Core:** Your core (your abdomen) needs to be tight while you're in a stance, as this helps you control your movements better. Research and practice different methods to tighten your abdomen without tensing your body.

- **Foot Placement:** Your foot is the base of every stance and must be placed correctly. With every stance, you need to stand on the balls of your feet to ensure even weight distribution and boost your reaction time.

- **Breath:** One of the ways to ensure that your body is relaxed is to breathe evenly; it makes it easier for you to maintain a proper stance.

There are several different stances in Taekwondo. Each Taekwondo association has its list of stances that must be mastered, and the following are basic ones that every student should know.

The Walking Stance

As the name implies, the walking stance looks like you are taking a step forward. The left foot is positioned forward and at an angle of about 30 degrees while the right foot faces straight forward. In this stance, the entire body is turned to about 45 degrees to the natural angle. This positioning aids balance. In most cases, your weight is evenly divided across both feet. The placement of feet in this stance makes it suitable as an offense.

The Horse-Riding Stance (Juchum Seogi, or Annun Seogi)

The Horse-Riding Stance

The horse-riding stance is similar to the positioning of one's leg when riding a horse. The specific placement of the feet varies depending on the style of Taekwondo practiced. In the Kukkiwon or WTF style, the feet are positioned at about two shoulder widths apart. The ITF style is less wide, at about one-and-a-half shoulder widths apart.

Both of your feet should point in a forward direction. The knees are deeply bent in an outward direction from your body. The extent of the bend required varies from one school to the other. In the horse-riding stance, there is an even distribution of weight between both feet. The hip is pushed forward, and the torso is kept straight and vertical. Your fists should be connected to the sides of your belt with the abdomen tight.

The horse-riding stance is used to help students build their leg strength and is usually used for exercising. However, the horse-riding stance may also be an offensive stance from where you can throw punches and kicks.

Back Stance (Dwi Kubi Seogi)

Back Stance (Dwi Kubi Seogi)

This style is also known as the L-stance in the ITF style. The back stance is also called the fighting stance in some traditional Taekwondo styles.

One foot is positioned in front of the other to do this stance. The foot at the back is placed in a perpendicular direction from the front foot. The positioning of the two feet should form the letter L.

The leading foot should be about one stride, around 3-foot, ahead of the rear foot. In the back stance, most of your weight should rest on your rear legs. The knees should be slightly bent, and both feet should be flat on the ground.

The naming of the back stance does not follow the normal convention in Taekwondo. Typically, the correct version of every stance implies that your right foot is the leading foot, and the left foot is behind. But for the back stance, this rule does not apply. In the right-back stance, the right foot is placed behind the other and is called the *trailing foot,* while the left plays the forward role.

Tiger Stance or Cat Stance (Beom Seogi)

Tiger Stance or Cat Stance (Beom Seogi)

For this stance, the front foot is placed forward with the heel slightly elevated, about 4-5 inches. This means that only the ball of your front foot should be placed on the ground. The rear foot should point outwards about 30 degrees.

Positioning your feet like this will shift most of your weight to the rear foot, and both legs should be bent at the knees. In the ITF version of this stance, your front foot should be forward by about a shoulder width.

Front Stance or Long-Forward Stance (Ap Kubi)

Front Stance or Long-Forward Stance (Ap Kubi)

This position is similar to the walking stance. In the front stance position, the forward foot is placed well ahead, up to two-and-a-half feet, of the rear foot. The front foot points straight ahead while the rear foot is positioned outward at an angle of about 25-30 degrees.

Your front knee is bent, and your shin is parallel to the floor. Typically, if you can still see the leading toes of your feet, then your knee is not bent enough. The rear leg is not bent, and the foot is positioned flat on the floor with no heel lift. The front leg bears most of the weight (around two-thirds) of your entire weight.

In this posture, there is a propensity to lean inward or turn the hips, but to accomplish it correctly, your hips must be held front to keep your body straight. These are the basic stances in Taekwondo. Learning and performing all the other moves will be much simpler if you have properly learned how to hold these stances correctly.

Blocks

Blocks are the most basic moves in Taekwondo. The goal of these maneuvers is to avoid being struck by an opponent. Almost any portion of the body can be used to deflect an approaching attack and strike an opponent.

Although a block is a defensive move, it also has to be strong and fast if you want to stop an attack. It is the purpose of learning this move from the early stages of mastering Taekwondo.

Each of the different block moves has a twist at its end to block the incoming blow effectively, and it takes a lot of practice to master the techniques for blocking. The middle block, high block, low block, knife block, and outside forearm block are all examples of block movements in Taekwondo.

- **The Low Block:** This is one of the most basic blocks to learn if you're starting Taekwondo. Position your fist on your opposite shoulder and sweep it downward in front of your pelvis; stop on the same side, near the base of your leg, as your blocking arm.

Low Block

• **Inside Block:** This is an inside sweeping motion used to protect the body by hitting attacks off to the side of the body. To do the inside block, bring the forearm of your blocking arm inside across your face or body to block an opponent's attack while stepping to the side.

Inside Block

• **Face Block:** To do the face block, shoot your arm up at an angle, stopping just over your brow. The move should be like you're forming a roof or church steeple. With this block, you can make a strike glance off you protecting your head. This type of block is excellent for weapon defense.

Face Block

- **Hand-Blade/Double Forearm Block:** This is a more complex block as it doubles as an attack move. To do this, one of your hands blocks the attack while the other is ready to deliver a follow-up strike to the opponent. There is a lot to this technique, and many beginners often misunderstand it.

Hand-Blade

Attacks

Initially, Taekwondo attacks only involved using the legs. The sport expanded throughout time to incorporate strikes and hits delivered with the arms. Attack maneuvers, on the other hand, are typically taught at higher levels of the sport since you can't learn to attack without first learning to defend. Punches have become an important weapon in Taekwondo, and thus, mastering them is crucial. Here are a few of the basic punch and kick attack moves you should be familiar with as a beginner:

- **Straight Punch:** To do the straight punch, the fist begins from the chamber of your hip and is thrust straight forward. The two big knuckles are used to make an impact. This punch should be delivered from the front stance or horse stance.

Straight Punch

• **Front Kick:** This is the foundation of almost all kicks in Taekwondo. Almost every other kick begins with a front kick chamber.

Front Kick

• **Knife Hand Strike:** This is often referred to as the karate chop. The attack is delivered down towards the outside with your palm facing downwards. It can also be done towards the inside with your palm facing up. The impact is made with the knife or meat of the hand. As an attacking move, the knife hand strike typically targets the side of the neck, trachea, or the opponent's temple.

Knife Hand Strike

• **Side Kick:** This is another very popular attack move in Taekwondo, and it is common for an individual's overall Taekwondo ability to be judged based on their sidekick. The sidekick is performed as a simple forward kick off the back leg. It requires you to bring your leg all the way to the side and thrust it forward at an opponent. This move can be a bit of a challenge to master.

Side Kick

• **Round Kick:** The round kick is also popular in many other martial arts, but the Taekwondo execution method is unique. On a back stance, turn your hips with your front foot as you bring your back leg knee upward. Kick your leg through to the target. It can be quite useful for sparring purposes.

Round Kick

Other Common Attack Moves

- Punching hand twists
- Double knife-hand strike
- Front kick
- Back kick
- Ax kick

Apart from these basic moves, many variations also exist to open the door to more advanced taekwondo techniques. The key to learning and mastering these moves is practice. The more you practice and improve your skills, you will execute these moves with greater confidence and scale up to more complex ones.

Chapter 5: Meditation and Taekwondo

Believe it or not, Taekwondo goes hand in hand with meditation. Meditation has been a very useful tool in the world of martial arts for years and always will be. Scientific research has proven that meditation possesses excellent health benefits, including but are not limited to:

- Decrease in insomnia
- Intelligence increase
- Reduced risk for illnesses
- Easy focus and concentration
- Increased personal development
- Lower blood pressure
- Reduced risk of cardiovascular diseases
- Lower stress and anxiety levels

Terrific right? It seems that meditation gives a much stronger and healthier body to whoever partakes in it. Meditation has all-around importance for everyone. Children use it to calm themselves before taking on that important math or calculus test. Adults with shyness or public speaking fears have been advised to practice meditation to calm themselves down before that job interview or presentation. Anyone in a stressful situation can calm themselves sufficiently through breathing and focus - two preeminent factors taught in meditation.

Breath and Focus

Meditation does a lot to improve Taekwondo performance, like giving you a much-needed energy boost that is beneficial for your training. For those new to meditation, the best way to begin is to focus solely on breathing. A few minutes of focused breathing goes a long way, and it is best to start with small steps and develop a good breathing pattern when accessing the inner self. Ensure to close your eyes while you're at it.

When immersed in Taekwondo, controlling your breathing pattern is of utmost importance because your movements require proper breath management. Taekwondo requires you to move with skill and precision. Of course, these movements are complex, but they must be done fluidly. Meditation training increases your lung capacity, which translates to better breathing patterns, and advanced meditation will fine-tune this further.

While performing Taekwondo movements, an unparalleled focus is needed. Focus is everything in Taekwondo, a miscalculation or slip-up can result in a loss for you, and one way to polish your focus is through meditation because it also utilizes one's focus. Consistent meditation gives your mind a rhythm that makes unparalleled focus effortless.

Many people erroneously believe that martial arts are all about physical strength. Even though the role of physical strength in martial arts cannot be underestimated, as it is very instrumental, there are several cases where a much smaller opponent overpowers a physically strong man or woman. Intelligence and focus take precedence over brute force in any situation. Most times, these biggies fall to smaller opponents due to the lack of a focused mind. Staying calm and focused during a fight allows you to execute the right movements with effective react time to your opponent's advances.

Mastering Meditation - Tips to Begin

We have outlined the excellent benefits embedded in meditation. It is a fact that Taekwondo athletes who incorporate meditation in their training outperform those who don't. So, how do you infuse it in yours?

Like anything else, there are several ways to meditate. As a beginner, twenty minutes of meditation practice per day should be good enough to get you started.

Find a quiet place. It's impossible to meditate amid a racket or a place steeped in noise and unhealthy sounds. Remember, your mind needs to concentrate. This quiet place can be anywhere - like your bedroom or office, for example; the important thing is that you must be uninterrupted. It shouldn't be a place where anyone can easily reach and disturb you. Most Taekwondo training clubs use the dojang. It's pretty powerful, and it's something you can take advantage of, too.

What's your intention with meditation? What are you looking to focus on at that moment? Or for the day? Meditation is about focus, and focus is about intentionality. You've got to be intentional about what you want to focus on. Do you want to perfect your techniques? Imagine playing both sides. Strategize. Meditation needs intention, or else the goal won't be achieved.

Start by breathing in and exhaling. Breathe slowly from the lowest part of your abdomen. Hold it in for as long as you can, then exhale slowly through the mouth. When you do this three times, your body enters a state of calm and relaxation, and so does your mind. Then, merely focus. Focus on your breathing and enjoy each breath so that random thoughts are lessened.

Your thoughts will undoubtedly be running around in your mind; this is inevitable; acknowledge them and let them saunter away. If you find yourself bogged down by too many thoughts, go back to focusing solely on your breathing until your timer goes off. You'll feel a lot calmer and more relaxed.

It's best to meditate with a timer. It helps keep you on track in case you lose track of time; this often happens when you get into the flow state. When this happens, twenty minutes feels like five minutes. Practice makes perfect, and as you meditate more often, you'll find it easier to meditate for more extended periods.

As a beginner, you have to learn to be patient with yourself and not engage in unnecessary pressure. Meditation differs for each one of us, and everyone responds to it differently. The one thing you must understand is that the flow comes with consistency. Meditation works best if and when it is done at the same time every day or regularly before Taekwondo tournaments or practices. Don't panic if you notice that you cannot meditate for long periods or your mind is always overwhelmed with thought processes. It doesn't always start out great for everyone. It takes time. As you harness the habit through consistency, you will become more proficient.

Understanding the Connection between Martial Arts and Meditation

Meditation embedded within fighting didn't begin today. It has been around from the beginning of time. Before participating in deadly fights, ancient warriors employed different breathing methods to soothe their minds and bodies. Meditation, on the other hand, did not become a part of martial arts until several decades later.

Traditional martial arts possess several philosophical concepts to improve the mental and physical capabilities of students. One of them is a calm mind and control over mental physique and emotions. These are crucial to carrying out and executing complex martial arts moves. There are distinctive breathing techniques that are recognized as meditation.

Martial arts training and competitions are not for the fainthearted. They are very stressful, and their intricacies are quite complicated, especially for beginners. If you are a newbie in the Taekwondo world, you can probably relate to consistent failure or struggle to suppress your anger on the mat when your opponent gets the better of you. This is why you need to meditate. It calms your mind and increases your concentration.

Meditation can take a person into a mental state known as The Flow State or Zone. Entering this state of intensive focus increases your fighting performance, changing how you perceive and understand pain; this will help you maintain a consistently high level of energy during fights. Listed below are three popular methods and exercises you can use to meditate before you jump into a Taekwondo session or training:

Breath and Body Control

Because of its ability to link the mind and body, a martial art such as Taekwondo does not discount the importance of breathing. When battling, you must inhale as you prepare to perform your move and exhale as soon as the motion is completed. You can pull off both defense and attack techniques by focusing on your breathing.

Deeper Meaning

Often certain things prevent a true martial artist from attaining his full potential. It could be a great and deep personal loss, the fear of death, or colossal injuries. To unleash the true fighting potential that invariably leads to excellence, the artist needs a comprehensive understanding of the world around him and his true self.

Self Defense Practice

This is all about awakening your subconscious and focusing on mentally integrating techniques you've previously learned. The goal is for your subconscious to have an automatic response. Although it sounds basic and oversimplified in context, it can take time to perfect.

Mindfulness and Taekwondo

"Mindfulness means paying attention in a particular way, on purpose, in the present moment, and non-judgmentally" - Jon Kabat Zinn

Mindfulness is one of many meditation techniques available, but it is especially important in Taekwondo. It requires you to deliberately pay full attention to the present without judgment or criticism. Practicing it formally requires you to set aside some time for it every day, informally requiring you to pay attention to what you are doing at any time of the day.

The good thing about mindfulness is that you can begin with the mundane - showering, dressing, eating, and so on. I'd recommend starting and mastering the informal practice before going on to the formal. Why? You get to start small and easy and then work your way up. The key is your attention and lack of judgment.

Now, do it formally. Find a comfortable position in a quiet place, close your eyes, and inhale. Let your attention be solely on your in-out breathing rhythm and nothing else. Your mind will wander around, and your senses will be heightened. Take note of your experiences but always return your attention to your breathing. In time, you will find yourself relaxing. Relaxation is important in Taekwondo, as sports psychologists and analysts have determined that anxiety is a huge cause of failure. So, the less anxious you are, the better. Your energy levels will also be regulated, but the focus is perhaps the most significant benefit of mindfulness.

Now with mindfulness, your mind is allowed to wander. But your task is to return your mind to your chosen focus of attention without judgment. When doing it, you will find that this exercise is perpetual. Distraction pops up, but you re-focus again and again. Eventually, you will gain the power to focus on what you want rather than what your brain wants. This focus is vital in Taekwondo because you must focus on your opponent's actions rather than emotions, like fear or doubt.

Conclusively, the greatest advantage of meditation in Taekwondo is its ability to aid you in breaking free from any fear, doubt, or shame as you step onto the mat with a clear mind and a single goal. It helps you learn and grow significantly and harness the pertinent factors to succeed. Since the beginning of time, it has been a part of the combat rituals of skilled warriors, and new trends, studies, and analyses keep emerging.

Not all coaches incorporate meditation into their teachings, but you will do well to engage in it consistently as a beginner. It will help you go a long way in your martial art success.

Remember, everything you want is on the other side of consistency.

Chapter 6: The 24 Essential Patterns in Taekwondo

Patterns in Taekwondo refer to the basic movements of both defense and attack in sequential order, against single or multiple imaginary opponents. Also known as Forms (teul), these patterns form an intricate part of Taekwondo training and are used to measure how far you've come as a student and the skills you have developed.

Patterns are taught and practiced for students to improve their knowledge of Taekwondo techniques, many of which are unique to Taekwondo. By practicing these patterns, you build flexibility and movement, improve your sparring ability, control of your breath, tone, and build of your muscles; you will also notice an increase in balance and coordination. These patterns are typically carried out in accordance with the books written by General Choi Hong Hi, the founder of Taekwondo.

Why Are There 24 Essential Patterns?

The 24 patterns of Taekwondo are based on the philosophy of Grandmaster General Choi Hong Hi. He thought that in order to obtain immortality and live a meaningful life, we should endeavor to leave a spiritual legacy to the future generation. The General opined that man's existence on Earth occupies a very short time in space, and he used the 24 patterns to represent this. In his legacy, he said,

"Here, I leave Taekwondo for mankind as a trace of man in the 20th century. The 24 patterns represent 24 hours, one day or all my life."

He created these core patterns to depict the life of man in just one day. The designs symbolize many significant events and well-known persons who affected the Korean people's history. Taekwondo has 24 patterns stretching across 19 to 72 movements.

Each of the 24 patterns carries a message that inspires you in your everyday life and when performing the movements. These synchronized movements range from simple to complex. The first ones are a combination of symmetrical movements executed with both sides of your body. Each pattern starts and finishes in the same location, allowing you to gain mastery over basic kicks and block techniques and develop a proper solid stance.

These patterns are also aimed at honoring Korean history and impacting each student with Korean historical knowledge and a full grasp of the Taekwondo techniques. Each pattern has a diagram and a specific number of movements that tell of an event or a heroic person in history. The stories chosen are realistic, and the struggles of each of the characters are relatable to people from other nations and cultures that are not Korean. The patterns in Taekwondo teach universal morals and inspire its students to strive for a life of legacy and devotion to a greater good.

The 24 Essential Patterns in Taekwondo

Chon Ji

The first of the essential patterns contains 19 movements that begin from a ready posture of parallel ready stance and end with left foot returns. It is translated as "Heaven the Earth." It refers to the history and creation of mankind and is usually the initial pattern a beginner learns in Taekwondo. The movements in this pattern are divided into 2 similar parts; one part symbolizes Heaven and the other, Earth.

Dan Gun

This is the next essential pattern. It is named after the man who founded the nation of Korea in 2,333 B.C. It involves 21 movements, requires a ready posture of parallel ready stance, and ends with a left foot return.

Do San

This pattern is named after the national Patriot Ahn Chang-Ho, who went by the alias Do San. He dedicated his entire life to Korea, fighting for its independence and educational rights. The pattern requires you to perform 24 moves, beginning with a ready posture of parallel ready stance and ending with right foot return.

Won Hyo

In 686 A.D., during the Silla dynasty, a monk named Won Hyo was credited with introducing Buddhism to the country, and this pattern was named after him. When performing Won Hyo, you make 28 moves, starting with a closed, ready stance, ready posture, and ending with right foot return.

Yul Gok

Famously dubbed the "Confucious of Korea," Yul Gok was a pseudonym of the 16th-century Scholar and Philosopher Yil. This Taekwondo pattern requires you to perform 38 movements that represent the 38th-degree latitude of the philosopher's birthplace. It starts with a ready posture of parallel ready stance and ends with left foot returns. The word "scholar" is represented by the graphic exhibiting this pattern.

Joong Gun

The sixth Taekwondo pattern is named after Ahn Joong Gun, a Korean nationalist who killed the first Japanese Governor-General following the unification of Korea and Japan. At the age of 32, he was imprisoned and hanged at Lui-Shung Prison in 1910. The 32 movements required of this pattern represent Joong Gun's age when he was killed. The pattern starts with a closed, ready stance and ends with left foot returns.

Toi Gye

This pattern was named after the pseudonym of the 16th-century renowned scholar and guru on Neo-Confucianism, Yi Hwang. For this pattern, you must perform 37 moves, starting with closed, ready stance B ready posture, and ending with right foot returns. The 37 movements indicate the guru's birthplace's 37th-degree latitude, and "scholar" is portrayed on the diagram for this pattern. **Hwa Rang**

During the Silla Dynasty in the early 7th century, a company of soldiers known as Hwa Rang Do was formed. This pattern was named after them, and to perform it, you are required to make 29 moves, beginning with a closed, ready stance C ready posture and ending with right foot returns. The 29 movements of this pattern represent the place where Taekwondo was fully developed as a martial art; the 29th Infantry division.

Choong Moo

This pattern was named after the reputed admiral of the Yi Dynasty, Yi Soon-Sin. In 1592, he was credited with the invention of the Kobukson, the pioneer armored battleship. His inventions are said to have paved the way for what is today's submarines. The pattern requires you to perform 30 moves, starting with a ready posture of parallel ready stance and ending with left foot returns. The last move of this pattern is a left-hand attack that represents how the great admiral died.

Kwang Gae

The Kwang Gae pattern is named after the famous 19th ruler of the Goguryeo Dynasty, Gwang-Gae-Toh-Wang. He is known for recapturing most of Manchuria and all other territories that were once lost. To perform this pattern, you need to form 39 movements, starting with a parallel stance with a Heaven hand-ready posture and ending with left foot returns. The 39 movements of this pattern represent the first two numbers of the year Kwang Gae started ruling, 391 A.D. The diagram for this pattern shows the territories recovered and consequent expansion.

Po Eun

Po Eun pattern is named after the pen name of a famous 15th Century poet and subject of the Koryo dynasty. He was one of the most important physicists of his time; he authored a poem, "I would not serve a second master though I may be crucified a hundred times," that is still widely known in Korea. For this pattern, you are expected to perform 36 moves beginning with a ready posture parallel stance with Heaven's hand and ending with left foot returns. The diagram for this pattern shows Po Eun's unending loyalty to his country and the ruler of that time.

Ge Baek

This pattern requires you to perform 44 movements, beginning with a ready posture of parallel ready stance and ending with right foot returns. It was named after Ge Baek, one of the most famous generals of the Baek Je Dynasty in 660 A.D. The general's military discipline is depicted in the diagram of this pattern.

Eui Am

Eui Am refers to the alias used by the leader of the March 1st, 1919, Korean independence movement, Son Byong Hi. The pattern requires you to perform 45 moves beginning with a ready posture of closed, ready stance D and ending with right foot returns. This pattern's 45 movements correspond to Byong Hi's age when he transformed Dong Hak to Chong Kyo (Oriental Culture to Heavenly Religion) in 1905. The diagram of this pattern showed his insurmountable character when he led his country.

Choong Jang

General Kim Duk Ryang, a Yi Dynasty general in the 14th century, was given the pseudonym General Kim Duk Ryang. It requires you to perform 52 movements starting with a ready posture of closed, ready stance A and ending with left foot returns. The final movement of this pattern is a left-hand attack that represents the untimely death of the General in prison. He was 27 years old.

Ko Dang

Ko Dang pattern requires you to perform 45 movements beginning with parallel stance with a twin side elbow and ending with right foot returns. It was named after the alias of one of Korea's national patriots, Cho Man Sik. He devoted his life to the independence movement of his country and fought for the education of Koreans. The 45 movements of this pattern represent the last two digits of the year Korea gained freedom from the Japanese: 1945.

Juche

Juche is the philosophical view that man is the ruler of the world and consequently his destiny. That is, man has authority over everything in this world and determines his path. This concept came from the Baekdu Mountain, which is supposed to reflect the Korean people's spirit. Performing this pattern requires 45 movements ending with right foot returns. The diagram of the Juche pattern symbolizes the Baekdu Mountain.

Sam-IL

This pattern represents the historical period of the Korean Independence movement that began on March 1st, 1919. To carry out this pattern, you need to perform 33 movements, starting with a closed, ready stance C ready posture and ending with right foot returns. The 33 movements of this pattern symbolize the 33 pioneer patriots who organized the independence movement.

Yoo-Sin

This pattern requires you to perform 68 moves, starting with a ready posture of warrior ready stance B and ending with right foot returns. General Kim Yoo-Sin, one of the Silla Dynasty's leading Generals, is the inspiration behind this design. The warrior stance B ready posture represents a sword drawn at the right side instead of the left side. This portrayed the General's error in obeying the King's instructions to fight alongside foreign forces against his own nation. The last two digits of the year Korea was united, 668 A.D., are used as symbolism throughout the 68 movements.

Choi Yong

General Choi Yong, the 14th century Koryo Dynasty Commander-in-Chief and Premier of the Armed Forces, has an influence on this pattern. He was well-liked and respected for his sincerity and devotion. He was assassinated by a number of his subordinate officers, commanded by General Yi Sung Gae, who went on to become the first emperor of the Lee Dynasty. This pattern requires 45 moves to complete correctly, beginning with a closed, ready posture C and concluding with right foot returns.

Yon Gae

Yon Gae Somoon was a well-known General during the Goguryeo period; this pattern was named after him. To perform this pattern, you need to perform 49 movements beginning from a ready posture of warrior ready stance A and ending with left foot returns. The 49 movements correspond to the year Yon Gae forced the Yang Dynasty to flee Korea after destroying over 300,000 of their warriors at Ansi Sung. It was the year 649 A.D.

UL-JI

This pattern requires you to perform 42 moves starting with a parallel stance with an X-back hand-ready posture and ending with left foot returns. It was named after General Ul-Ji Moon Dok, who is credited with defending Korea against a nearly one-million-strong Tang invasion in 612 A.D. Using hit-and-run guerilla tactics, the General was able to annihilate a substantial portion of their forces. This pattern's schematic is in the shape of an "L," which represents the General's surname. The 42 movements of the pattern represent the age of the author who designed the diagram.

Moon-Moo

The Silla Dynasty's 30th King, who was buried at Dae Wang Am (which translates to Great King's Rock), inspired the Moon-moo Taekwondo pattern. The King requested that his body, after his death, be placed in the sea so that he could protect his country from Japan. The Sok Gul Am (Cave Stone), a noteworthy artifact of Silla Dynasty culture, was created to protect his grave after he was buried. This pattern necessitates 61 movements, which correspond to the last two numbers of the year Moon Moo attained the throne, 661 A.D.

So-San

This pattern calls for 72 movements, beginning with a closed, ready stance, ready posture, and ending with left foot returns. Choi Hyong Ung, a 16th century Lee Dynasty monk, was given this pattern's name. The pattern's 72 movements indicate the monk's age when, in 1592, he and his student Sa Myung Dang assembled a battalion of monk soldiers to resist Japanese pirates on the Korean Peninsula.

Se Jong

This pattern is named after Se-Jong, the great Korean King and a renowned meteorologist credited with inventing the alphabets of the Korean language in 1443. To execute this pattern, you need to perform 24 moves, starting with a ready posture of closed, ready stance B and ending with left foot returns. The 24 movements depict the 24 letters of the Korean alphabet, while the "Z" diagram for this pattern symbolizes the King.

Tong-IL

This pattern requires you to perform 42 moves starting with a ready posture of parallel stance with an overlapped backhand and ending with left foot returns. It symbolizes the union of the Korean nation that has been separated since 1945. The diagram of the pattern is shaped as "I," signifying a uniform and single race.

Important Tips to Note When Performing Taekwondo Patterns

You are expected to start and end each pattern at the same location. It shows how accurate you are in performing the pattern.

- You must maintain the correct posture and face correctly at all times.

- You need to ensure your muscles are either tensed or relaxed at the crucial and precise moment when performing the pattern.

- You must perform each pattern with a rhythmic movement that is void of stiffness.

- You need to ensure acceleration and deceleration of patterns per the instructions given.

- You must perfect each pattern before moving to the next one.

- As a student, you are expected to know the purpose of every movement.

- As a student, you are required to perform every pattern with realism.

Chapter 7: The Five Tenets of Taekwondo

If you have attended any standard Taekwondo class in the past, then you must have heard this phrase at some point. The tenets of Taekwondo are often recited as part of the Taekwondo student oath in most schools. At the beginning of class, the pupils recite the oath, either in unison or by repeating after their instructor.

The Taekwondo student pledge serves to remind students of their responsibility to themselves, the art, their instructor, their fellow students, and society. So, the tenets form an integral part of the oath that students are expected to be familiar with.

Luckily as a beginner reading this book, you can become acquainted with them earlier than most. More than just learning how to fight, you get to understand some of the fundamental ideas of the sport and appreciate them.

To begin, we need to understand what a tenet is. A dictionary or an encyclopedia defines a tenet as an opinion, dogma, principle, or doctrine that a person or an organization believes, practices, and maintains as true.

An encapsulating definition, perhaps, but it does not do justice to the rich history and heritage from where Taekwondo tenets were derived. The point is to understand the role of these tenets. They were created to give the ancient warriors powerful motivations, and the same remains true as the driving force behind all the learning processes, even today.

- Courtesy
- Integrity
- Perseverance
- Self-Control
- Indomitable Spirit

These are the five tenets of modern Taekwondo, but they haven't always been like this. The old tenets of the ancient art were known as the Hwarang code of conduct and comprised of five rules. They have the same meaning as these modern ones but are written in a more flowery and superfluous language. The Hwarang code is:

- Rigid loyalty to the King and country
- Respect and obedience to one's parents
- Unswerving loyalty and trust to friends
- Display of courage and never retreat in battle
- Prudence in the use of violence and taking a life

While connecting how one came to become the other would be tricky, it's easy to see their similarities. Respect and obedience are synonymous with courtesy. Loyalty and trust are a significant part of integrity. Prudence in the use of violence and killing is self-control. "Display of courage and never retreating" shows perseverance and an indomitable spirit.

As always, Taekwondo stays true to its roots.

The five tenets are a source of guidance to serious students of the art. They are a moral code and must be adhered to, not merely every time you're in the dojang, but every time you use the skills. Taekwondo is spiritual philosophy, and it is just as much of a mental discipline as it is a physical one. Your success in understanding the mental part of Taekwondo will also determine your physical success.

Respect for the rich history and tradition of Taekwondo must always be freshly embedded within the mind. It is why most coaches and instructors will recite all the tenets once the students have bowed on the mats to remind students that Taekwondo revolves around self-improvement and humility. The greatest thing about the tenets of Taekwondo is that they can serve you in your everyday life, too.

Analyzing the Tenets

Courtesy (Yah Yie)

Courtesy is another word for politeness and humility and enduring respect for oneself and others. It is immense consideration for others and is usually seen and displayed in the dojang. Shoes are removed in the dojang as a sign of respect for the training facility, and students bow to the Grandmasters and Black Belts to demonstrate respect for their accomplishments. Whenever the Grandmaster or instructor is giving a lesson, students must remain silent and listen actively; side discussions symbolize disrespect. If you are a beginner who has never been inside a dojang before, you must remember these things.

Often as students progress through the ranks and become friendly with their tutors and seniors, complacency about courtesy creeps in, which is when vigilance is required. Being friendly is great, but being a perfect embodiment of one who adheres to the tenets at all times is even greater. Courtesy also requires respect without seeking gratification. Sometimes, students are courteous only to their seniors for what they can get, but never courteous to newcomers; this is unacceptable.

The truth is that your dedication to the tenets will not be tested at your inception stage. It is easy for a beginner to adhere to them, but as you gain more expertise, you will need more self-awareness and understand the necessity of constantly renewing your dedication. It isn't surprising to see young artists courteous when they are at the lower rung of the ladder only to attain the black belt status and turn into what no one recognizes.

Integrity (Yum Chee)

Integrity is steadfast adherence to a strict moral and ethical code. Taekwondo has its ethics, and instructors, grandmasters, black belts, students, and beginners must all adhere to them. For instance, instructors must teach or demonstrate techniques that are deliberately harmful to the student's opponent. Even when students are taught the bone-breaking moves of self-defense, emphasis is placed upon the principle that they are only executed when the use or threat of force is life-threatening.

As a budding martial artist, you must recognize that integrity is one of the virtues you must hold dear. You must learn to be true to yourself, your dojang, your Grandmaster, and your training institute. Understand that moral codes and ethics are as important as learning Taekwondo techniques. In Taekwondo, integrity also means staying true to your word. You are a beginner today, but one day you'll evolve to the point of teaching others. How will you handle it? You must be able to teach and willingly help those who need help. Integrity means respect and loyalty. It means staying true to your word and yourself. It means defining right and wrong and listening to your conscience.

Perseverance (Inn Nae)

An old Asian Proverb says: Patience leads to value or merit. Perseverance is a trait needed for the growth process, and, as a beginner, it cannot be more strongly emphasized how important this is for you. Taekwondo is a complex sport, and you cannot be weak at heart and hope to excel in this sport. Learning to perfect your techniques – polishing them until they gleam – is only attainable by perseverance. *Those with black belts didn't get there by chance!*

Perseverance at a task is in itself a skill. As you progress within Taekwondo, you will discover your unique set of strengths and weaknesses. There will be certain moves you'll find easy to perfect and others not so easy. But no matter how tough or arduous the process is, you must learn to be persistent and dedicated to never giving up on perfecting your flaws. Perseverance is the one tenet that will lead you to excellence and give you a sense of fulfillment when you achieve what you have worked assiduously for.

At all levels, you have to renew your dedication to perseverance. There will be times when you feel safe and assured about certain moves you think you have perfected, only to receive a rude awakening at a training practice or, even worse, during a tournament. It is perseverance that will drag you back to the mat and ensure you refine and fine-tune what you thought you knew.

As a beginner, the best way to handle the steep learning journey is to take it one day at a time. For every day you show up, strive to be better than what you were yesterday. When you constantly have that principle at the back of your mind, you'll be more proficient at Taekwondo until you become top-notch.

Self-Control (Kook Kee)

Taekwondo is a combat martial art that features foot strikes, kicks, and punches. It requires you to learn how to control yourself because it's very easy to cross the line. Imagine, for one instance, that you become a black belt, and you're sparring with someone you intensely dislike. It could be tempting to beat them to a pulp by executing flawless moves, and yeah, that could make you feel good about yourself, but that's not what Taekwondo is about. A lack of self-control can prove to be disastrous for the opponent and student.

Self-control is also about paying attention to your instructor and not moving an inch until you are instructed to. It means maintaining your calm while your opponent trashes you hard. It means you respond well to criticisms no matter how angry they make you. Besides Taekwondo, all martial arts require years of understanding and patient practice. If you have no self-control, you wouldn't be able to last.

Indomitable Spirit (Back Jok Bool Kool)

Taekwondo is all about self-improvement. Whenever you find the terrain difficult, remind yourself why you began training in the first place.

Have you seen the epic movie, Troy? It starred Hollywood Powerhouse actor Brad Pitt as the legendary Greek warrior Achilles. In the first battle where the Greek army advances, Achilles and his Myrmidons singlehandedly take on the fearsome warriors of Troy at the beach. They were resilient enough to take down a city that had never previously been conquered.

Let's use a more martial arts example. Remember the movie "Karate Kid"? (Fun fact, the movie should be called "Kung Fu Kid" because Dre Parker actually learns Kung Fu and not Karate). During the tournament, Dre was badly wounded and was told his injury was so bad that it was advisable to quit fighting, yet he persisted because he was determined to conquer his fears that night.

One final movie reference to drive home the point; do you remember the battle movie 300? Leonidas and his army of 300 Spartan warriors faced the powerfully superior army of Xerxes and displayed one of the most profound acts of courage the world has ever seen. Their epitaph reads: Here lies 300, who did their duty.

These movies are used as examples because they are warrior movies. Even if you are a beginner, you must understand the day you decided to step onto the mat in a training center; you became a warrior. And as a warrior, you must show courage, even in the face of overwhelming odds.

Perseverance is the physical effort required to face challenges, but an indomitable spirit is the will of the soul that is necessary to conquer the opposition. You display an indomitable spirit when you consistently choose to rise above the fears gnawing at your heart. You display an indomitable spirit when you choose not to be weak-willed and face your opponent without fear. You display an indomitable spirit when you choose to keep competing at tournaments, even though you have lost so much. You display an indomitable spirit when you have trouble mastering your moves, but you don't stop showing up for practice. You need a fighting spirit to succeed in life, and Taekwondo is not an exception.

Contemporary martial artists largely ignore the five tenets of Taekwondo, even though they're chanted like a mantra in school. It might be tempting to do the same, and you might even meet those who tell you that these tenets are old-fashioned. Yet, be assured with all confidence that adhering to these tenets is a sure guarantee of success.

Additionally, these tenets can serve you well in life. Self-control teaches you how to keep cool under fire. There is a saying that you can regret the harshness of your words after your anger dies, but you can never regret the silence you kept. Integrity will help you keep your word and stay loyal in your relationships. Courtesy ensures that you respect everyone, including strangers. Perseverance and an indomitable spirit will give you immense willpower and courage to attain whatever dreams you have outside Taekwondo.

Taekwondo isn't just a combat skill. It's a life skill, too. Living by the five tenets helps you become not only a better fighter but a better human being. It gives you the physical and mental discipline to improve all areas of your life. The tenets can fit in effortlessly with any religious or philosophical beliefs you might have. So, study the five tenets and let them be a source of guidance throughout your martial arts journey. It will be one of the best life-changing decisions you'll ever make.

Chapter 8: Taekwondo Hand Techniques

Most people believe Taekwondo is a martial art that is all about the kicks, and they aren't entirely wrong. But, while kicks were a predominant staple of the sport at its onset and still remain an integral part of it today, there are a variety of hand techniques also still commonly used. This chapter focuses on some of the hand punches you will learn in Taekwondo and tricks and strategies to improve them.

Throwing the perfect punch in Taekwondo, like in any other martial art, takes time and practice. You must learn how to execute each technique correctly in order to obtain the necessary skills; it will give you an edge, especially in competitive matches.

There are several hand technique combinations in Taekwondo. Some are more popular than others, and the complexity also widely varies from one technique to another. Here are a few things to know about Taekwondo hand techniques.

Punches Are a Secret Weapon

Punches are mostly underutilized in Taekwondo, especially in competitive games. Most people focus on kicks without paying enough attention to their hand skills. This could be an advantage for an opponent who invests their time and effort in developing hand techniques.

Not only do people forget to throw punches, but they also hardly defend against them. It is quite interesting considering you can earn between 1 to 2 points for landing a punch, depending on the rules of the competition.

The Mexican national Taekwondo team takes advantage of this. They are currently one of the top teams globally and have dominated for more than two decades. You'll notice that their performances incorporate more punches than most, which contributes to their dominance in the sport - further proving that you can stack up valuable points with punches if you know how to apply your hand techniques correctly.

How to Throw a Good Punch in Taekwondo

Contrary to popular belief, you need more than just your hands to throw good punches. Many hand techniques in Taekwondo require you to use your entire body. In addition to your hands, your arm, abdomen, and feet can contribute to the effectiveness of your punch.

• **Your Feet:** In Taekwondo, your feet are your solid base and foundation. You must be as stable and balanced on the floor as possible to generate enough power for your hand technique. Most moves require you to stand on the balls of your feet to stop, turn, and pivot your punches properly.

• **Abdomen:** This is the center of your body. In all physical sports, including Taekwondo, the abs serve the purpose of connecting your hands to your feet. Power generated from your feet is transmitted to your hands, so you need to learn to tighten your core to ensure you're not losing the power behind your punch.

• **Arms:** While most hand techniques in Taekwondo involve the hand, the arms are equally important since they do the movement. Your fist and wrist must be at the correct level of firmness during a punch to avoid injury.

Taekwondo Hand Techniques

There is an assortment of punches and hand techniques in Taekwondo; below are some of the most popular ones.

The Jab

This method is employed in Taekwondo for both defense and distance measurement. The jab can also be used to bait an opponent, leaving them vulnerable to a counterattack. The jab is designed to provoke your opponent into attacking while you counter with a kick. The jab is delivered as a direct blow from a distance, with your arm over your leading foot. This technique should be executed with speed and timed explosiveness if you want to catch your opponent off guard. It is typically accompanied by a slight rotation of the hips and torso. The fist is rotated at a 90 degrees angle through the punch, becoming horizontal on impact.

Bring the lead shoulder up to guard your chin while the hand is completely extended; the other hand remains next to your face to guard your jaw. Retract your lead hand into a guard position in front of your face as soon as you make contact with the target. Instead of only striking with your hand while throwing jabs, transfer some of your body weight into your punch to sustain the blow. For maximum effect, aim for a 10 to 15cm hit behind the target surface. When in combat, try to strike through your opponent rather than merely making contact on the surface.

As a note of precaution, you should ensure that your wrist is in proper alignment when you deliver a jab. You risk an injury if it bends on impact, especially against a solid surface.

Straight or Cross Punch

A straight or cross punch is similar to a jab, but instead, you strike the surface or opponent with the rear of your hand and not the forward fist. Because you have to twist your body into the strike when delivering it, a straight punch normally has more power than a jab.

You strike your opponent with the first two knuckles of your fist when doing a cross or straight punch. Depending on the rules of the competition, it might be hurled towards the head or the body. When your opponent is approaching you, straight punches are the best option.

Uppercut

Uppercut

The uppercut is a strike that involves moving your first in an upward motion while striking an opponent. Turning your torso upward to load the arm and shooting your hands upward to hit an opponent is how this punch is accomplished. In a close fighting situation, an uppercut is best employed to land a body shot on your opponent. For maximum effect, your shoulder must be lowered along with your knees. Then, propelling your body upward and forward, you extend your fist towards the opponent's chin and face.

Hook Punch

It's a more compact or shorter variant of the standard straight or cross punch. It is usually thrown with the front hand and targeted to an opponent's sides. When delivering the hook punch, your body makes a slight tight turning movement.

Hook Punch

In Taekwondo, the hook punch is considered a more controlled and effective alternative to the more traditional haymaker punch. Use this punch to land a body shot in close combat or to get beyond an opponent's guard; it's also more difficult to parry a hook punch.

You can use the hook to lead a cross punch or as part of a combined sequence of punches, with the last being the hook. The hook is also effective as a counter strike against an opponent. Push into your hook punch with your leading leg and perpendicularly turn your foot while throwing the punch to give it more strength.

Back Fist

In Taekwondo, there are different types of back fists. The most common type is performed with your front hand, similar to the jab. But in this case, the padded part of your backhand is used. At the end of this punch, flick your hand as it hits the side of the opponent's head (depending on the organization, hitting with the padded end of your hand may be prohibited).

Back Fist

There are two versions of a back fist in Taekwondo; the Turn Back Fist and the Spinning Back Fist. The difference is very subtle.

The turn back fist; Before striking an opponent with the back of your hand, the hand should be rotated around 180 degrees.

The spinning back fist; there is a 360-degree spin of the hand. This type of punch typically follows another strike that initiates the spin. Both types of back fists are typically set up with a punch or kick.

Hammer Fist

To perform the hammer fist technique, make a motion similar to if you were swinging a hammer. With the fleshy part of your hand, you should execute a downward motion. The hammer fist can be used to attack above an opponent's guard and can also be thrown off a spin or turn for extra impact.

Hammer Fist

Swing your fist downward towards the target to execute this technique. One major advantage of the hammer fist, especially for beginners, is that it is quite safe, and there's no risk of injury to your hand or knuckles since you hit the target using the bottom padded part of your fist.

Extended Knuckle Punch

An extended knuckle punch is a variation of the traditional fist configuration used to deliver a normal punch. To throw an extended knuckle fist, one finger protrudes forward (usually the knuckle of the middle finger). The knuckle is used to generate the impact, concentrating more force on a smaller area for a greater impact.

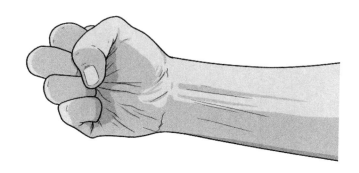

Extended Knuckle Punch

The extended knuckle is often used to attack the pressure points. The technique takes its roots from traditional Kung Fu. However, it is considered a high-level Taekwondo move only used by advanced students because it requires a level of accuracy and conditioning most beginners don't have.

To deliver this punch right, you are expected to relax your body as much as possible during the strike and tense it right at the point of impact, relaxing it again when recoiling your hand. The sequence of relaxation and tensing the body helps to attain the highest possible velocity while also achieving a maximum transfer of force.

Spear Hand Strike

The spear hand strike is an open hand strike. Aptly named because the hand is fully extended, giving it the appearance of a spear. The strike is delivered with the tips of the fingers and is usually targeted at the eye, throat, or other more sensitive targets. One significant advantage of this technique is that it extends the range of the hand by a few inches.

Spear Hand Strike

Note that the spear hand strike must be used with caution. If you miss and hit a hard target, you risk injuring your fingers. Also, while this technique is commonly taught in Taekwondo, it is considered illegal in tournaments.

Ridge Hand Strike

The Ridge Hand Strike is another common open hand technique. When executing this punch, your hands and fingers are extended while you strike the target with the thumb side of your open hands.

This strike is quite effective; it is delivered in the same manner as a hook or overhand punch. However, to prevent injury, you are expected to tuck your thumb into your palms to avoid injury when you hit the target.

Differences in Hand Technique Rules between Taekwondo Organizations

There are different rules regarding the various hand techniques in Taekwondo. The WTF, ITF, and ATA each have specific rules about which punches are allowed and what body part is off-limits.

World Taekwondo Federation (WTF): Martial arts fighters are only allowed to strike in straight blows using the knuckle area of their hands, according to WTF guidelines. In addition, punches can only land on the abdomen, truck, or uppercuts; hooks are not permitted.

International Taekwondo Federation (ITF): The ITF's rules for hand punches are similar to the WTF's, with the exception that the ITF allows hits to the head. In addition, the ITF permits contestants to throw a variety of blows rather than just straight punches.

American Taekwondo Association (ATA): The rules for ATA sparring are comparable to those of the WTF. Only straight abdominal blows are legal.

Tips for Improving Your Hand Techniques in Taekwondo

Consistent practice and training are needed to sharpen your Taekwondo hand techniques. Like everything in Taekwondo, the more you practice, the better you get. It is also important that you understand your hand techniques' philosophy of push and pull and hard and soft execution.

The principle of push and pull has a major impact on the delivery of your punches. When you push your punching hand forward, you must pull the non-punching hand backward with as much power you are pushing the punching hand. The same principle applies to blocking. When you block, pull the non-blocking hand with equal power as the other hand to maximize its full potential.

Additionally, it's imperative to master how to be soft and hard in various aspects of your technique. Being completely hard is not good, and conversely, all soft is also not great. Finding the sweet spot between both ends of the extreme is essential. A martial artist must learn to relax before executing a technique and tense up just at the right moment to focus all of his power behind a punch for maximum effect.

As mentioned earlier, hand techniques involve your entire body and not only your hands. Everything from your feet (your lower energy center) to the tip of your finger has to be involved in delivering a blow. Your hip is used to crack that whip to generate enough power and speed for your blows.

Also, you must have safety considerations in mind for each hand technique and pay proper attention to them. You can risk a sprain, dislocation, or even breaking your hand if your hand strikes are executed ignorantly.

Exercises to Improve Your Hand Techniques

There are different methods of training you can use to improve your hand techniques. Three of the most common ways to boost your punches include:

- **Train with a Punching Bag:** Taekwondo schools usually have a punching bag you can use to train. To strengthen your hand techniques, your coach should lead you through sessions of bag practice.

- **Mitt Training:** Another method that instructors use to assist with this practice is to use a punching bag. It requires teaching pupils how to synchronize punches while holding mitts for them to hit. Conditioning training is also conducted with this technique.

- **Technical Sparring:** Students are sometimes paired with a sparring partner, encouraging them to practice various hand techniques on one another. Note that Taekwondo punches and strikes are best practiced under the supervision of your instructor.

Chapter 9: Taekwondo Foot Techniques

It is no secret that Taekwondo boasts some impressive kicks. They are called Chagi in Korean, the most recognizable aspect of the sport. Taekwondo kicks can be performed through a variety of methods, including jump kicks at various heights, spin kicks, or a combination of these. The type of kick to be used depends on the specific situation. While some kicks are great for self-defense, others are more suitable for attacks in competitions. This chapter looks at some common Taekwondo kicks, what they're used for and how they're executed.

The Front Kick ("Ap Chagi")

The front kick, also known as the flash kick or snap kick because of how fast it is executed, is among the first sets of kicks you will learn as a beginner. It is a powerful kick useful at both beginner and advanced levels of the sport.

When executing a front kick, you raise the knee of your kicking leg high to your waist level. Then, move your foot forward towards the target; this exerts a forward force that pushes the target backward. The front kick can be used to inflict significant damage.

With any Taekwondo kick, the resting or off leg is just as important as the kick itself during execution. For this kick, you bend your off-leg slightly to execute the kick. Your weight should be rested on the ball of your foot and not flat on the floor. You may also lift your foot slightly off the floor but be careful not to overdo it. During the kick, the off foot rotates slightly away from the target.

The position of your arm and torso are important, too. Bring your fist up towards your chest as in a blocking position. As the kicking leg is brought forward, the arm on that side should be brought downward and pulled back.

In WTF and ITF styles of the sport, the toes are bent upward when executing this kick to ensure that you strike the target with the balls of your feet. In some other styles, the toes are pointed straight in the same direction as the rest of the foot. This way, the topside of your foot is used to hit the target. In this style, the reach of your leg is also extended.

The Side Kick ("Yeop Chagi")

This is another move that you'll probably be expected to learn early on in your Taekwondo career. The sidekick is also a powerful kick that can have different implications depending on the Taekwondo rules you are following.

To perform this kick, you need to raise your knee while also rotating your body about 90 degrees. You then exert force by straightening your leg. When executing this kick, you should pivot your non-kicking foot on the ball so that it is fully turned away from the target at the moment of impact.

Your torso must be bent to one side during a sidekick; this is particularly important if you are doing a high sidekick. If you're kicking with your right leg, your right arm lowers down behind your kicking leg as you kick it forward. The left arm is pulled to the chest area with the fist closed in a blocking stance.

As with the front kick, the part of the foot used to hit the target depends on the Taekwondo rules you are following. But the options are either between the outside edge of your foot and the heel.

The Roundhouse Kick ("Dollyeo Chagi")

The Roundhouse kick is arguably the most referenced Taekwondo kick in pop culture. This kick is very powerful when mastered. To perform the roundhouse kick, the knee of your kicking leg is raised and aimed towards the target. Next, you pivot the balls of your resting foot and turn your hip slightly; this will turn your body sideways towards the target. Then, straighten your leg, moving the shin parallel to the ground as you kick.

In some versions, the top of your foot is the striking surface for this kick. In this situation, you hold your ankle straight to align with the rest of your leg and point your toes along the same line. In other versions, the kick is executed with the balls of your foot. If this is the intention, your ankle and toes should be bent upward.

Your non-kicking leg is a vital part of the roundhouse kick. It propels your body as it rotates to turn your side towards the target. It is important that you pivot on the balls of your resting foot. Typically, the non-kicking foot must be turned away from the target at the moment of impact.

When you turn to do the roundhouse kick with your right leg, you have to bring your right arm down to the right; it provides counter-rotation to your kicking leg. Some people prefer to bring the right hand behind the right leg at the moment of impact.

The Back Kick ("Dwit Chagi")

One of the more complex Taekwondo techniques is the back kick. As the name implies, you have to perform this kick by setting yourself up away from the target. Do this the wrong way, and you will end up losing your balance or falling over.

To execute the back kick, you have to pivot away from your opponent and execute a kick linearly backward once you are facing away from the target. It is important to note that although many people refer to this kick as the Spinning Back Kick, the kicking leg does not make a spinning motion, and the spin only refers to how the martial artist turns their body during the kick.

Your torso should lean slightly forwards as you execute the kick to increase the height of this kick. Also, turn your head to the side as you execute the kick so that you can see where you are kicking.

The Outer/Inner Crescent Kick ("An Chagi / Bakkat Chagi")

There are two variations of the Crescent kick; inner and outer. They are also commonly referred to as the inside and outside crescent kicks. Both variations involve forming an arc; in one, the arc goes from the inside to the outside, and from the outside to the inside in the other variation.

Both types start the same way, with you raising your leg and bending it like you're about to do a front kick. The knee is then pointed to the target's left or right side. When the snap's energy is deflected, your leg whips across the target in an arc, striking from the side.

This move is great for aiming for an opponent's defenses – striking the head or knocking down their hands before launching a close attack.

In the case of an outward crescent kick, the arc forms at the center of your body and moves outward. You kick the target with the blade (outside edge) of your foot in this manner.

For the inward crescent kick, the arcing motion begins from the side of your body and gradually moves inwards to the center. This way, the kick is executed with the inside edge of your foot.

The Hook Kick ("Huryeo Chagi")

The hook kick is a newer Taekwondo technique. In execution, it is just like the roundhouse kick but with a twist. At the end of the kick, when the foot is extended, there is a backward sweeping motion as your leg impacts the target creating hooking motion.

When doing the hook kick, strike the opponent with the heel of your foot (or the flat of your foot when sparring). The start of the hook kick is similar to the sidekick. You raise your kicking leg's knee forward towards the target, whereupon you pivot your off foot to the side, moving your kicking leg's hips over.

When kicking past the target with a hook kick, you consciously angle your leg towards your kicking foot toes. By the time your leg hits the target, it is extended a little to the side. Your heel strikes the target at full extension, then you bend the knee while in position and snap it to the side.

Typically, the back of your heel is used to deliver a hook kick, but at a closer range, the back of the calf or back of a bent knee may also serve to strike.

The Ax Kick ("Naeryeo Chagi")

This is another very recent addition to competitive Taekwondo. As the name implies, executing this kick is similar to the motion you make when bringing down an ax to cut a log of wood. You begin by raising the ax above your head and swinging it down towards the log (at a slight angle for better impact).

The Ax Kick

The ax kick works the same way. You pull your leg down by exerting a downward pressure while keeping your heel directed down to the ground after raising it high up towards an opponent. Any area of the body above the torso can be a target area for this kick, including the torso, head, collarbone, or shoulder.

The ax kick is different from the other kick in its execution. While most other kicks involve bending your knee first, this is not the case with the ax kick. Instead, your kicking leg is held straight as it is raised (slightly to the side of your target) and brought down forcefully.

Like the crescent kicks, there are two variations for the ax kick. It is called the inside-outside ax kick if your leg is raised towards the center of your body and brought down slightly outside as you do your downward strike. In contrast, if the kicking leg is raised towards the outside of your body and brought down slightly in the center, it is an outside-to-inside ax kick.

The Knee Strike ("Mureup Chigi")

If we're strict with the definition of the word, then the knee strike isn't exactly a "kick." However, the knee is an essential part of any good kick and executes a powerful blow on its own when used correctly.

The Knee Strike

The knee strike can be done in a variety of ways. Even yet, the main premise is that they all require getting the opponent into the knee or driving the knee towards them. Knee strikes are more prevalent in mixed martial arts (MMA) and other kinds of martial arts. In Taekwondo, a knee strike is directed at the head or body of your opponent. To execute this move, you must control your opponent's body or head and bring the knee forward. Simultaneously, the knee is raised to strike at the opponent. When making this move, keep your striking leg's ankle straight (pointing downward).

The Scissor Kick ("Kawi Chagi")

This is a more advanced kick performed by jumping up into the air. The scissors kick is not commonly used in competitions or even for self-defense because of its complex execution. Instead, it is reserved for demonstrations.

The Scissor Kick

Executing the scissors kick involves jumping up to execute a kick that hits two opponents simultaneously, and each leg is used to target an opponent. Of course, this is a very impressive move if executed correctly, but hardly practical in a combat situation.

Flying Side and Back Kicks ("Twi Myo Yeop Chagi / Twi Myo Dwi Chagi")

These two kicks are perhaps the most legendary in Taekwondo. They are an advanced version of the sidekick and the back kick, with the key distinction being that they're performed while "flying."

To understand how this kick works, it is important that you understand the distinction between a jumping kick and a flying kick.

The term "flying" is often used to indicate that the martial artists' body has significant momentum when performing the action. To perform a flying kick, the martial artist needs a running start to generate enough momentum for the kick.

For instance, for the flying back kick, you run forwards towards the opponent, rotate your body 180 degrees so that you are facing away from the target then deliver the kick. The flying back kick is delivered linearly, meaning the leg does not arc as it makes its way towards the target, and instead, it is thrust directly at the target while still in midair.

The flying side kick and flying back kicks are mainly used in demonstrations than in actual combat situations, but they may sometimes be used in sparring.

Tips for Improving Your Kicks in Taekwondo

To add more power and speed to your kick in Taekwondo, you must work on increasing your muscle strength. A combination of exercises, a stretch routine, and consistently practicing and perfecting the technique of your skill will help boost your form and ensure the proper execution of your kick techniques.

Exercising Your Vital Muscle Groups

However, first, you must become familiar with the main muscle groups that determine the strength and speed of your kicking techniques. Your quads, calves, abs, lower back muscles, and lateral obliques play an important role in your execution of the various Taekwondo kick techniques.

Targeting these muscles during your workout routines will improve your performance since they make up an interconnected network that contributes to the overall results of your kick in Taekwondo. If any of the links in this connection is missing due to an error, weakness, or injury, it will be impossible to reproduce a Taekwondo skill with the right speed and power. Therefore, your training routine should include specific exercises that target each of these muscles to prevent this. The goal is to improve the strength and flexibility of each muscle to boost overall performance.

Exercises for the Quads

The quadriceps are made up of four muscles that coordinate movement. Squats, leg extensions, and lunges are ideal exercises for targeting these muscles in particular. The good thing is that you can do these workouts in your home with no need for specialized workout equipment. You can also boost the intensity of these workouts in your home or public gym with barbells, dumbbells, kettlebells, and other weights.

Hamstrings

You need your hamstrings for foot rotation during a kick. The strength of your hamstrings is also crucial for achieving the hip extension and knee flexion required for good kick execution. Excellent exercises that target this muscular group are lunges, glute and ham raises, and deadlifts. Squats and kettlebell swings are also beneficial for increasing explosive power.

Calves

Most people believe that the calf muscles have a minor role in kick production. However, they are missing out on a lot. They are an important part of the interconnected chain, and without them, your kick will be weak. Some workouts you can do to boost their strength include step-ups, calf raises, and lunges.

Abs

Your core muscle is the center point of the body, and you need a strengthened core not only for kicks but also for punches and blocks. In almost every martial art, including Taekwondo, emphasis is placed on core strength, and routines like pushups, deadlifts, pull-ups, and crunches are often recommended for stronger abs and core muscles.

Lower Back

Your lower back carries a lot of weight when performing kicks. Strengthening your lower back boosts the power and speed of your kicks and prevents strain and other injuries. To develop your lower back muscles, try exercises like pull-ups, chin-ups, face pulls, pullovers, and dumbbell rows.

Lateral Obliques

This muscle group is particularly important for executing turn and spin kicks. Because they demand a lot of lateral flexion and trunk rotation to produce optimal outcomes, techniques like these rely on the lateral oblique. Exercises such as lateral pull-downs and side planks are excellent for strengthening your lateral obliques.

Stretching Exercises and Taekwondo

Most kicks in Taekwondo require you to be as flexible as possible for proper execution. Therefore, to master the art, you must include a stretch routine in your training regimen because it boosts your muscle flexibility. Stretching exercise also helps to condition your muscles and prevent injury.

However, it's imperative not to go straight to stretching workouts. Before you begin stretching, you should complete a short warm-up session to get your blood flowing properly. Warm-up for 3-5 minutes;

you can include shadowboxing or jump-roping before beginning stretch activities.

Pull Down Stretch

One of the most typical stretch exercises for increasing flexibility is the pull-down stretch, which is also relatively basic. Reach down to the floor while maintaining your legs at shoulder width. Try holding this position for about 10 seconds before moving your hands from one side of your body to the other.

Crouching Stance

Lean over to one side of your body with one of your knees bent to one side, and the other knee is kept straight. Try holding this position for about 10 seconds before shifting to the other side and repeating the same procedure. Do this for both sides of your body about 2 or 3 times.

Horse Stance or Ready Stance

This stance has been explained extensively earlier in this book. The horse stance is halfway between a squat and a lunge. To maximize the stretch's tension, keep your back vertical, draw your chest out, and push your legs outwards while pushing your hands outwards. Hold this position for 30 seconds to one minute.

Splits

Splits are common in martial arts, and Taekwondo is not an exception. It is included as part of the practice in almost every Taekwondo school. Do a split for about 30 seconds (or more if you can hold it longer). You may not be able to do splits properly at first, but if you follow a stretch regimen, you will eventually be able to execute it.

Stretch Kicks

Stretch kicks are more difficult to master since they require you to emulate the actions of a kick. Begin at your hip, then gradually raise your leg higher until you are good enough to kick up to your head level.

Other Exercises to Increase the Speed and Power of Your Kicks

Run a Few Miles

Good old running can help build your muscle strength and improve your performance. You should run for roughly 4-5 miles at least three times a week if you're an athlete who is serious about your performance. However, you don't have to travel that far straight away; you can start with 2 miles and work your way up.

Swimming Works Too

Swimming is a terrific way for martial artists to get a proper body workout. It builds your muscles and is also a great way to boost your endurance. It can be used as an alternative to running or done in addition to your routine.

Box Jumps

This exercise requires you to move in swift and explosive motion. Workouts like this are great because you need that explosive energy behind your kick. Try doing 5-10 reps of box jumps up to 3 to 5 times. You can do this at a comfortable height so that you don't over-exert yourself.

Practice Your Kicks

If there is anything you should often do often, as a martial artist, you should practice. The more you practice, the more refined your kicks will be. Practice throwing your kicks to master them. Daily practice is recommended.

Tips for Effective Kick Practice in Taekwondo

It should be noted at this point that repeated practice does not do much good if your technique is bad. Your brain will only end up memorizing the wrong moves. Since muscle memory serves a lot in executing kicks in Taekwondo, correctly practicing them will give better results than when you merely practice without paying attention to form or the accuracy of your techniques. Here are some helpful tips to improve the effectiveness of your Taekwondo practice.

Learn the Proper Technique

Every Taekwondo move has a specific sequence of movements that must be followed for maximum effect. It's also a good idea to use the correct techniques to avoid injuring yourself.

Set Up Your Kicks Right

As mentioned earlier, a big part of this is the setup; it's about getting your technique right. If you continue to throw uncontrolled kicks, you may wind up losing your balance; not setting up your kick right can lead to serious injuries.

Maintain a Stable Base

To achieve the desired power and speed with a kick, you have to maintain a solid base throughout the entire move. For instance, always stand on the balls of your feet instead of flat-footed, and it will allow you to drive enough force into the ground to throw your kick with maximum speed and power.

Angles Matter

Kicks appear faster than they really are if you angle them right. If you master how to angle your kicks, you will add more speed to them.

Don't Try to Match Your Opponent's Speed

Take this advice for when you are sparring with an opponent that is a faster kicker than you. The worst thing you can do is try to match their speed. You will always trail behind because you are slower, and that's an almost certain defeat.

So, what can you do? It is recommended to go for the one thing you have control over, which is strategy. In the absence of speed, wisdom is your only shot at beating a faster opponent. If you can strategize properly, you will be able to observe your opponent's movement and time your move to counter or block them more effectively.

It is important to note that the list of kicks in this chapter is not an exhaustive one. There are several other types of kicks in Taekwondo that you should become familiar with. They are included in your syllabus, and you will learn them gradually as you move from one level to the other. Of course, learning the kicks is only half of the battle. You have to master them and learn how to boost your speed and power. For this, you will need the tips covered in this chapter to improve your kick training and strategy in a sparring situation. The more you're willing to put in the effort, the stronger and faster your kicks will get.

Chapter 10: Self-Defense in Taekwondo

Self-defense is one of the major reasons people become interested in learning martial arts in the first place. At some point in everyone's life, we are faced with a life-threatening situation, and some are unlucky enough to encounter these situations more frequently than others. Learning a few basic self-defense techniques will prepare you mentally and physically to deal with intimidating situations so that you are not entirely helpless in dangerous situations.

Of course, Taekwondo is one of the most popular forms of martial arts worldwide that is learned for this very purpose. Although it was once a brutal form of martial arts, it is no longer practiced that way in modern times. Today, people learn Taekwondo for tournaments and to defend themselves in difficult situations.

Taekwondo has various attacking techniques and blocking moves that are very handy for self-defense purposes. Its efficiency is proved by the fact that it was used in Korean and Vietnam battles for self-defense. It is a fighting style that is fun and easy to learn; still quite relevant today.

Even though Taekwondo is now being taught as a combat sport, it can be applied for self-defense; one only needs fine-tuned active thinking in self-defense combat scenarios. The type of Taekwondo training you get depends on the martial art school you attend. Some schools specifically include Taekwondo training against an armed attacker, multiple attackers, or when at a disadvantage in their lessons. For example, you are with a child or an elderly person. When your attacker has a weapon, the whole scenario changes entirely. Any careless move could leave you with serious injuries or may even cost you your life. At times, self-defense involves the need to identify and make use of improvised weapons. You are taught how to react and defend yourself in bad situations against an attacker, regardless of whether a mugger, thief, or stranger harassing you.

When you train consistently and correctly, you reach a point where Taekwondo becomes natural, and your body reacts to attacks instinctively.

Importance of Taekwondo Self-Defense

When you have adequately trained in martial arts, your self-respect and confidence are boosted. Walking down that unavoidable lonely street alone or defending yourself from a mugger does not sound all that scary to you anymore - well, at least, not as much as it used to.

The more you train, the more confident you feel about your capabilities, your self-esteem is enhanced. Even more pivotal to how you react, you feel less terrified in times of danger. Your newly attained confidence can also be applied to other specific areas of your life, like work. It is one of the best things about self-defense in Taekwondo. Your increased self-confidence makes you feel empowered and in control of certain situations in your life, and your mental strength plays an active role in successful defense fights.

Taekwondo can also help to improve concentration, self-discipline and develop a solid, strong will. As your training sessions intensify, you will notice that your ability to focus and observe even the tiniest details increases.

Taekwondo lessons are repetitive. Consistently repeating the same move over and over again until perfection is attained requires a lot of self-discipline. Like your self-confidence, you can intentionally apply your improved self-discipline and concentration skills to other areas of your life for more productivity. Mainly, you apply these skills to relevant situations instinctively, especially when you have trained hard, and Taekwondo has become part of you.

Self-Defense Techniques

"Hosinul" is a term used to describe Taekwondo self-defense mechanisms. With hosinul, you can quickly disarm your opponent and restrict his movements. The theory of self-defense techniques in Taekwondo is that you should be able to take out your attacker with a single move. However, a significant period is needed to require the skills to achieve this feat.

Short-range, long-range, and ground rage attacks are also important techniques to master for defense because you're never sure which style your attacker will use against you when. A deficiency in any of these techniques could put you at a great disadvantage.

The size, stamina, and aggressiveness of your attacker are also important factors to consider during the confrontation. Furthermore, the type of training you've had, your dedication to practice, the ability to read your opponent, and attack timing are also essential. Consistent training and body conditioning practices are key success determinants in fights; they determine how effective Taekwondo is in actual combat.

You Only Need the Basics

You need to devote yourself to mastering the basic techniques consciously. Advanced techniques, though they appear elaborate, are not suitable for self-defense fighting in a real-life situation. They leave you more prone and open to attacks and are not practical in actual fights. Your primary goal in a defense fight is not to show off your fancy fighting skills but to defend yourself and get away from threats as soon as possible.

You have to learn how to use the right move combinations to your advantage. While practicing or going through drills, focus on carrying out the moves correctly. Some of the key techniques you need to learn are: Joint dislocation, break boards, throwing powerful kicks and punches, hand strikes, and elbow and knee strikes. It is also necessary to know how to locate pressure points and use them to your advantage.

You must have invested enough time in Taekwondo to know that it focuses on kick techniques even though arm strikes are biologically faster. The idea behind this is that, since your legs are stronger and longer than your arms, they are more effective during fights. This notion is quite valid when you have trained so hard that you can move your legs as fast as your arms.

Another very important thing to note is that it is not advisable to use blocks against kicks in self-defense. If you are going to use it at all, it must be your very last resort because blocking against powerful kicks could easily cause injury to your hands. The best way to avoid attacks is to be well versed in evasive techniques, as they allow you to easily avoid incoming attacks from your opponent and conserve strength to counter-attack from their blind spots.

Basic Taekwondo Moves That Are Useful for Self-Defense

Kicks

Like punches, there are also different types of kicks used for specific purposes. Powerful kicks can keep your attackers at a safe distance from you. For example, for swift recovery during battle and to properly deliver attacks to your opponent's lower body, use the forty-five kick or the roundhouse kick. Round kicks are very versatile moves. The advantage is that this move can be used near an opponent and at a distance. They can cause your enemy to lose strength in their ribs, legs, or any other place you decide to attack. Attacks are even more efficient when you combine roundhouse kicks and punches to an enemy at close range.

Front and push kicks are useful in pushing your opponent away, and they are effective when you want to move an attacker away from your escape route. Defensive sidekicks are powerful kicks that serve the dual purpose of countering incoming attack kicks and causing pain to your opponent. A hard fast kick to the groin is a good way to incapacitate your opponent.

Straight Punches

There are different styles to throwing an efficient punch. Punches differ based on the technique used and the amount of power being applied. It is therefore essential to learn and know the appropriate time to throw a particular punch. An efficient punch in a specific scenario may be useless and irrelevant in another. A straight punch is particularly effective in Taekwondo because it is hard and quick, and it is quite difficult to detect and evade straight punches. Usually, your attacker is not prepared for it, so you get more chances of knocking him out fast. The combination of straight punches, front kicks, and low blocks are good building blocks in self-defense combat.

Your Fighting Stance

The stance is one of the most important things to get right in a fight situation. They differ according to various styles and techniques, and a proper fighting stance ensures that you are protected from dangerous openings and avoidable attacks. With the fighting stance, you stand with your feet firmly placed on the ground at shoulder width and ensure you are well balanced. Keep your chin down and your hands up, ready for an attack. Your stance should be flexible enough to allow for a quick attack, counterattack, and defensive movements.

Elbow and Knee Strike

You might need to use every part of your body in self-defense situations, especially if you don't have a weapon. Even your elbows can come in handy here. Most people are unaware of how much damage can be caused by an elbow during a fight. Striking someone's head with your elbow, or being struck in your head by an elbow, can be quite painful. You can cause excruciating pain to your attacker when you grab his head and hit him with one clean elbow strike. Knees strikes are just as effective, too. It must be noted that you need to stand firm and well balanced to land a proper knee strike. Never launch a knee attack into an open space. It could leave you vulnerable to attacks or counterattacks; it is advisable to pull your opponent in before you use your knee strike.

Hand-Blade Block

This move is also commonly known as the double forearm block. With this move, one of your hands blocks an attack while the other hand is ready to block the next incoming attack.

Palm and Face Blocks

Instinctively, you usually raise your hands to protect your eyes, face, and head during a provocation from strikes. Palm block lessons are good at reducing injury without sparing you any composure or balance. They also help you get ready for a successful counterattack.

Knife Hand and Back Fist Strikes

The knife hand strike is mainly targeted against your attacker's trachea, neck sides, and temples, used with the palm facing outwards or inwards. The back strike is quick and used to attack the head or the gap between the nose and the upper lip.

Palm Heel Strikes

These strikes are great for hard attacks without causing serious injury or damage to your hand. A palm heel strike is a perfect option if you are not too eager to break your hand or bruise your knuckles in a fight. So, you don't need to worry about severe damage or pain to your hand as you deliver hard attacks to your opponent in a self-defense situation using this strike.

Footwork

Sidestepping is a defensive footwork move and is great for performing counterattacks and dodging blows. It's a skill that takes time and effort to master. Skip movements come in handy when your opponent makes use of the whole leg length, such as in a situation where your opponent is armed with a knife, and you can move in and out of his kick range, kick your opponent, and disarm him.

Self-Defense Techniques in Different Situations

In situations where you need to defend yourself, lower your expectations; maybe your attacker will not be fair. So, to save yourself, there is absolutely no need to stick to the rules you adhere to in class and tournaments. For instance, punches to the body and a full-force kick to the head are not allowed in some competitions. But, when it comes to life-threatening situations, no one cares if you stick to the rules or not. In fact, you put yourself at a disadvantage when you adhere to some rules. Here are a few common attack examples used in a confrontation and how to defend yourself as a beginner.

Frontal Choke

In this type of attack, your attacker is trying to squeeze your neck from the front. Use the knife strike to hit your opponent in the chest around the ribs to distract them. Open block with both hands and strike your assailant on his neck.

Collar Grab

When your opponent does this, you can discontinue the grab by forcefully moving one of your opponent's hands down and raising the other. Then you can deliver an elbow strike to his chin.

Shoulder Grab

Grab the opponent's attacking hand and hold his elbow with your other hand. Widen your stance for balance and press the hand down to incapacitate your attacker.

Rear Shoulder Grab

In a case where your shoulder is grabbed from behind, the first thing you should do is keep your shoulders relaxed. Look behind and raise your arm to circle your opponent's elbows, locking them tightly in place. You can then deliver a strike to the rib cage area with your other free hand.

Hair Grab

When the opponent grabs your hair from the front, move to the side and palm block the attacking hand. Then, deliver a hard punch to the stomach of your attacker. Your fast response determines how efficient this counterattack will be.

Linear and Circular Taekwondo Self-Defense Techniques

In Taekwondo, the techniques can be grouped into Linear and Circular categories of movement.

Linear Techniques

Also referred to as Hard Techniques, this group consists of direct strikes, punches, kicks, and head butts. These moves need great strength for proper execution. Your technique choice largely depends on the distance between you and your attacker. If your opponent is very close, the use of your knees or elbows would be your best bet. If he is a little bit more distant, make use of punches, and use kicks when your attacker is out of arm's reach. Your attacker should be taken out with a single attack with the proper technique, especially when you are faced with more than one opponent.

Circular Techniques

This group is also labeled as the soft techniques. The moves in this category are mostly circular, as indicated in the name. Circular moves largely depend on delivering counterattacks to your opponent. This category of techniques is a more defensive approach, and a lesser amount of strength is needed than direct linear attacks.

The circular technique aims to redirect the attacks of your opponent and put you at an advantage. In other words, when your opponent attacks, you carry out a circular motion to throw him off balance and manipulate the attack, so your attacker is forced to be destabilized or remain in a lock position, giving you an edge over him. Then you have the chance to apply the finishing move.

Chapter 11: The Art of Blocking in Taekwondo

Blocking is the act of deflecting or halting an opponent's assault from making contact with one's body in Taekwondo and other martial arts. A block usually entails putting a limb across the attack line. However, even though blocks are the most direct sort of defensive technique in martial arts, they are not the only ones. Other evasive strategies include evasion, trapping, and slipping, all of which are referred to as "soft" or evasive techniques. When blocking, you are expected to relax your body as much as possible prior to the block but tense your muscles just enough on impact. It is then followed by recoil and relaxation after the block is completed. This cycle of relaxation and recoil ensures that the block achieves the greatest possible effect. The relaxation gives the blocking limb good velocity, while rigidity at the point of impact ensures an optimal transfer of force.

Basic Principles of Blocking

When doing a block, several basic principles must be observed to ensure your safety and to maximize the effects. Here are a few:

1. Keep your arm bent at an angle of about 15 to 45 degrees. This way, you intercept the attack at an oblique angle rather than head-on.

2. Do not extend your blocking arm beyond the point of focus of the attack

3. At the moment of impact of the attack, lower your blocking arm slightly

4. Besides a few exceptions, always withdraw your blocking arm immediately after making contact with the attack

5. At the contact point of the attack, the blocking arm forms a triangle with the attacking arm.

How Blocks Are Classified in Taekwondo

There are different types of blocks classified based on the relative position of the blocking hand, the facing posture, type of blocking tool, and the method of the block, as well as the purpose of the block, of course.

Classification of Blocks Based on the Blocking Level

Blocks can be classified as high, middle, low, inward, or outward based on the orientation of the blocking motion you make during the block.

High Block (Nopunde Makki)

A block is considered a high block if your fist reaches the same level as your eyes at the moment of impact. A high block is used to intercept an attack directed at an area close to or above your neck. You can execute a high block from nearly all stances. This block can be performed as a forearm block, knife hand, reverse knife-hand, palm, side fist, or double arm block.

Middle Block (Kaunde Makki)

If your fist or fingertips reach the same level as your shoulder during a block, it is considered a middle block. This type of block is used to fend off an attack directed at your solar plexus and any area above it. Like the high block, the middle block can be executed from any stance. The middle block involves the hand and the foot. The side sole, foot sword, side instep, ball of your foot, and back sole can play a vital role in executing this block.

Low Block (Najunde Makki)

A low block is used to intercept an attacking hand or foot directed at your lower abdomen or an area below it. Your blocking hand or foot must take the impact from the attack at the same level as the target area. You can perform a low block with your outer forearm, reverse knife-hand, palm, or side sole.

Inward Block (Anuro Makki)

If your blocking tool meets the attack with an outward to the inward trajectory to your chest lines, this is called an inward block. You can execute this type of block from any stance. An inward block is used to block an attack directed towards your chest line. This block can be performed with any blocking style except the backhand and inner forearm.

Outward Block (Bakuro Makki)

When your blocking tool hits the target from an inward to an outward trajectory, it is considered an outward block. This block can be performed from any stance, but you cannot execute an outward block with your palm.

Front Block (Ap Makki)

A block is considered a front block if your body is facing the target fully and your blocking tool is at the center of your body. The front block is performed from any stance regardless of the initial position of the opponent. You can execute a front block with your outer forearm, twin palm, knife hand, or your palm.

Side Block (Yop Makki)

A side block is when your body faces your opponent at the point of executing a block. It is executed from any stance regardless of the position of your opponent. A side block can be executed with any blocking tool and is often focused on the center of the defender's shoulders.

Other Ways Blocks Are Classified

A block can be classified based on the height of the block, the position of your hand, orientation, and so on.

Classification of Blocks Based on Hand Position

Several modifiers are used to name blocks based on how your hand is positioned during the execution, often mentioned in the section above. Some common hand positions used to execute a block include knife hand, ridge hand, palm heel, and so on.

Classification of Blocks Based on the Orientation

It is possible to refer to the hand's direction when the block is executed to describe it. Whether your palm is up or down when executing a block determines the side of the forearm that serves as the blocking surface. In a conventional outside block, for example, the blocking surface is your outer forearm, which means your fist is palm-down as you execute the block. Conversely, if the inner forearm is used, the fist is palm-up when executing the block.

Classification of Blocks Based on the Position of Your Off-Hand

For most types of blocks, the default position of your off-hand should be in a direction opposite the motion of the block. This opposing motion contributes to the action-reaction effect, which is one of Taekwondo's key principles. However, in some situations, your off-hand may be included in your block. Here are several examples:

• **Support Block:** Your blocking arm should be resting on your off-arm in this situation.

• **Assist Block:** The block is deemed an assisting block if your off-hand offers an additional push to the blocking arm.

• **Augmented Block:** If the off-hand is near the blocking arm and not drawn back, your block is strengthened.

It is important to note that these different descriptions of the blocks are not always consistent and may vary based on the organization standard that is applied.

Common Blocks in Taekwondo

In this section, we will briefly go over some common blocks in Taekwondo. While most of the blocks listed here are basic, some advanced ones that require high-level technique are also included.

The Outer Forearm Block (Bakat Palmok Makgi)

The outer forearm block can be done in three different ways: high, middle, or low. To complete this block, your forearm should snap forward in a horizontal frame. Impact with the attacking force is made with the outside of your forearm. In a walking stance, this type of block is frequently used. Typically, you begin your block in a ready stance and transition to the walking stance as you execute the block.

Inner Forearm Block (An Makgi)

This is the opposite of the outer forearm block in that it is performed with the inner forearm. You take a step forward and move your arm in a chopping motion. The arm is held vertically with the palm facing inward, and the blow is delivered to the interior of the arm.

Rising Block (Chookya Makgi)

A rising block is a high block that is used to defend against blows to the head and shoulders. Raise your arm over your head horizontally and let the inside of your forearm take the blow. In circumstances where your opponent has a weapon, this block is also useful for self-defense.

Guarding Block (Daebi Makgi)

In the ITF style of Taekwondo, a protecting block is more often used. The guard block is commonly executed in an L-Stance or as a rear foot stance. Your forehand is pushed forward to meet the opponent's hit at the point of impact with the offensive force, while the resting hand is placed on the side of your chest. In this position, the guard hand should provide sufficient cover for most of your body.

Twisting Block

A twisting block occurs when your torso turns in the direction of the strike. One of the biggest advantages of this block is that you can subsequently grab your opponent. The knife hand twist block is created when this block is combined with the knife hand.

Scissors Block (Kawi Makgi or Gawi Makgi)

The scissors block is a combination of a downward block and an outer forearm block. Both actions should be done simultaneously, with both arms producing a scissoring motion across your chest. The scissors block allows you to protect different parts of your body simultaneously with a single move.

Cross Block or X Block (Otgoreo Makgi)

In the ITF Taekwondo style, the cross block is also referred to as the X-fist block. Cross your wrists in front of your body on the same side as your leading leg, palms facing outwards. Using your fist or knife hand, you can defend against high, middle, and low assaults.

Palm Block (Sonbadak Naeryo Makgi)

This block entails putting your open palm in front of your face to shield it. For a proper palm block, all of your fingers should be linked rather than stretched out. When you meet an attacking punch or kick with a thrusting motion, the recoil will keep you from hitting yourself in the face.

Single Forearm Block (Wae Sun Palmok)

The single forearm block can be used to block kicks directed at your torso area. Your lead hand is aimed at your opposite shoulder, while your other arm is swiftly lowered downward to meet the opponent's kick. The forearm is used to perform this type of block.

Twin Forearm Block

This is a version of the single forearm block that is used to defend against both high and intermediate attacks at the same time. You usually start with your arm crossed across your chest. Then you execute a high block with your outside arm and a middle block with your inner arm.

Double Knife Hand Block (Yangsonnal Momtang Magki)

The double knife hand block is identical to the outside block, with the exception that it is executed with a knife hand while standing in a back stance. This move can be used to block a high or low attack.

Double Forearm Block (Doo Palmok Makgi)

This block is comparable to the forearm block that most people are familiar with. But, for this move, you place your supporting hand behind your blocking hand, giving the blocking arm extra support. It also makes it easier to block a secondary attack if necessary.

Nine Block (Gutja Makgi)

The nine block is a more complex blocking technique for defending your midsection against a variety of attacks. The name of this blocking technique is derived from the hand's position when you're executing this block. The nine-block is usually executed in a walking stance.

Push Kick (Mireo Chagi)

Although the push kick is not strictly speaking a block, it can still be used to deflect an opponent's strike; hence it being included in our list. Bring your knee to your chest and thrust your leg outwards at your opponent. It will not only deflect your opponent's strike but will also provide you with ample room to counterattack.

Cut Kick

The cut kick, like the push kick, can be used to deflect an opponent's attack. It has the appearance of a sidekick and is frequently employed to counter spinning blows during a sparring bout. If your opponent executes a spin kick, throw a cut kick at their hip or lower back to knock them off their feet. The cut kick also gives you enough room for a counterattack.

Mountain Block (Santul Makgi)

This is a more popular move in the WTF style. It is used to block multiple attacks directed at your face simultaneously. The inside edge of one wrist moves clockwise while the outside edge of the other wrist moves in the opposite direction when performing this block.

Tips for Practicing Your Taekwondo Blocks

The various Taekwondo blocking techniques described in this chapter are easy to execute, and there are many other variations of each of these types. As with every other aspect of the sport, the key to improving your blocks in Taekwondo is practice.

To practice your blocks, you can either do so on your own by practicing different Poomseas (patterns) or by practicing with a sparring partner. When training on blocks with a teammate, you should alternate taking turns practicing specific blocks. If your partner takes an attacking position, you take the defense and vice versa. During practice, attacking kicks and punches should be thrown at less than half their regular speed to allow space and time to perfect your block.

When practicing the Poomseas of your blocks alone, do so in front of a mirror. This way, you can observe if you're performing the blocks correctly and placing your hands in the proper position.

There is an extensive library of blocking techniques in Taekwondo. As you go through the various levels, you will be taught some of these blocks.

Chapter 12: Stretches and Drills

Taekwondo is a portmanteau of many things - martial arts, defense mechanisms, a pathway to a more energetic and enriching life experience, and a rich combination explosion of Chinese and Korean traditions. However, at its core, it is a weaponless traditional fighting skill that emphasizes jumping kicks, head-high kicks, sidekicks, and striking. The average Taekwondo lesson includes kicking drills, striking drills, and speed targets. These drills are engineered to improve motor skills and flexibility.

Taekwondo has bountiful physical fitness benefits. Research shows that it dramatically improves cardiovascular health, boosts athletic ability, and improves balance and coordination. In 2014, researchers found that Taekwondo athletes exhibited good endurance, upper-and-lower body strength, increased flexibility, and anaerobic power. These benefits are also products of good drills and stretches.

Since it is a physically defensive art, drills are usually combined with other calisthenics exercises and more strength and conditioning drills to provide a complete workout. They are advantageous because they boost your ability as you continually advance further. There are distinctive ways to stretch. Stretching often follows a warm-up to activate cold muscles. A warm-up is necessary because cold muscles do not stretch well. Some Taekwondo sessions are also concluded with stretching. The idea is to take advantage of the fact that all the muscles are warmed up fully at that point. Let's take a look at the importance of stretching before analyzing the various types.

Importance of Stretching

• It increases flexibility. The body needs a good deal of flexibility, but it is more pertinent for martial artists, especially in the hips, lower back, and legs.

• The range of motion is also increased. Good stretching helps you attain higher kicks or become better at challenging moves or positions.

• Fewer injuries usually occur during training and competitive matches when your muscles are conditioned through stretching.

• Often, stretching plays a role in injury recovery. Physical trainers make use of gentle stretching after injuries to restore flexibility and strength to the body.

• It increases blood flow and enhances muscular development. Stretching also enhances mental focus because of how much concentration it requires. Many artists use it as a meditation of some sort.

• It reduces muscle soreness after workout sessions and gives better motion flexibility, which helps you punch or kick well and move as fast as lightning.

• Stretching helps prevent injuries because it allows a full range of motion when performing Taekwondo techniques without pulling or tearing up the muscles. Taekwondo requires excessive use of the legs. When you stretch properly, it allows you to put your legs in proper positions without straining too much. It is impossible to achieve this with tight muscles, and incorrect moves can lead to nasty injuries.

• Since stretching gives more flexibility, your muscles become less and less resistant to fighting movements or positions. The result is a burgeoning speed that improves your performance. Enhanced speed paves the way for greater power, and better flexibility and range of motion improve your overall performance as a Taekwondo warrior in speed and power.

Stretching must be done properly and consistently. It is a key component of any sport, but it's more important for Taekwondo due to the explosively defensive nature of the sport. As a beginner, understand that stretching only on training days is dangerous. Stretch on non-training days at home to increase your flexibility as fast as possible.

Work with the pace your body demands; otherwise, you could be dealing with complicated injuries. But if you only stretch on your training days, your flexibility will be slow to improve, and you will be frequently outperformed by those who prioritize stretching. While stretching at home, consider doing it in the morning rather than at night.

Different Kinds of Stretches

Note: As a beginner, it's best to do these stretches with your instructor or trainer first. Most martial artist instructors are professionals with finely tuned experience. Some of the stretches below are risky, so only attempt them at home when you have a good grip and understanding of what you are doing.

Standing and Sitting

• **Neck Rotation:** Simply rotate your neck in a clockwise, circular motion. Another technique is to stand or sit with a straight back and stare directly ahead. Bring your arms in front of your body and straighten them, then clasp them tightly together. Turn your head so that your chin is above your shoulder. This stretch goes all the way from your jaw to your collarbone.

• **Neck Stretch:** Stretch your neck to the front and back and then to the side. Push or pull your neck to extend the stretching if you want to go further.

• **Shoulders:** Bend your arms so that your fists are near your shoulders and rotate your arms in clockwise and counterclockwise motions. To stretch your shoulders, hold an arm out straight and pull it to your upper chest using your other arm. Place your other arm just below the elbow of the stretched arm and squeeze it into your chest to further increase your stretch. The aim is to feel a stretch across your shoulder.

• To stretch the front of your shoulder, stand with your feet a shoulder's width apart and look straight ahead. Bring your hands behind your back and intertwine them while keeping your arms straight. Now gently ease your hands back, as far back as they will comfortably go, and squeeze your elbows toward each other.

- Stretching the back of the shoulder starts by standing with your feet a few widths apart and looking straight forward. Bring your arm straight up so that it's parallel to the floor. Bring your arm over your chest while keeping your shoulders down. Use your other arm to squeeze the arm into the chest by placing the forearm just below the elbow of the stretched arm.

Back Stretches

- **Lower Back:** Lie on your back on the floor with your knees bent. Pull your knees towards your chest. When doing this stretch, do your best not to arch your back.

- **Back:** Kneel on the floor and keep your knees firmly together. Put your arms upward, and then bend from the waist, fold your chest onto your knees and place your hands flat on the floor. Leave them out straight. Sit back on your heels after a while to feel the stretch seep into your lower back. For a backward stretch, bend as far backward as possible, looking backward over your head. Let your legs stand a shoulder-width apart and place your hands on your hips.

- **Kneeling Back Stretch:** Kneel on all fours. Look at the floor with your back straight. Arch your back upwards and let your head drop to the floor. Return to the starting position and drop your stomach (not your chest) towards the floor. Stay facing forward, and keep your knees and hands shoulder-width apart when doing this stretch.

For a partner backstretch, interlock elbows and stand back-to-back. Take turns lifting each other off the floor by bending forward.

Waist Rotations

Rotate your waist in a circular motion with your hands on your hips and legs at a shoulder-width apart. Careful to twist slowly. For a side stretch, bend your waist over to one side and then bend to the other. Try raising your arm over your head as you do this.

Besides waist rotations, a ball stretch is also required. Lie flat on the floor and grab both feet with the aim of pulling them over your head. The goal is for your feet to touch your forehead and hold it there for at least a minute.

Leg Stretches

Lie flat on your back, bend one knee and bring it up to your chest; finally, ease it towards your opposite shoulder. This gives you a stretch across your bottom from the top of your leg to your lower back. For your outer hip, lie flat on your back with your arms slightly outstretched. Bend one knee upwards, then grab it with your opposite hand and bring it across your chest onto the floor. Still, keep your other leg straight and your shoulders on the floor. The aim is to stretch the outer leg up to your hip.

An excellent stretch for your groin is to sit on the floor with a straight back with your legs stretched out. Spread your feet as far out as you can, keeping your legs straight. Maintain a straight back while lowering your chest to the ground and stretching your arms out in front of you. Go as forward as you can, then let your elbows hold the stretch.

When stretching the front of your thighs, stand on one leg and bring the opposite heel up to your bottom. Grab your foot and gently pull upwards.

For the back of your thighs, stand with your legs straight, and bring your feet together. Raise your hands above your head and fold yourself down, and try touching your toes.

Understanding Taekwondo Drills

Taekwondo is a weaponless defense mechanism, meaning that you rely solely upon your sparring skills to carry it out safely and effectively. Sparring is at the core of Taekwondo, and the most important thing is to always infuse control and not let it get out of hand. If you are scared of getting hit or injured or doing even hurting another person, this doesn't mean Taekwondo isn't for you.

Your fears are understandable because the human body possesses a strong in-built sense of self-preservation. However, drills were designed to aid you in your sparring. So, to succeed in tournament combat or mat training sessions, you must learn to work more effectively on your sparring skills. Sparring is a fight without actually fighting; it helps you develop a wider understanding and spurs the development of skills such as speed, distance control, and power.

Before starting any drills, the first thing to do is to have an open space of about 100 square feet (10 feet wide and 10 feet in length). It will be more than enough space to accommodate you if you are training alone and at home. But as a beginner, it's better to start drill practice at a training center to have a partner for the drills.

Shadow Sparring

Shadow sparring is usually performed in front of a mirror. You will need to throw kicks, punches, and elbows; you will also need to use proper footwork as you maintain a good range in your flow motion. The good part about shadow sparring is that you can see yourself, so you can easily identify your flaws. But, if you are shadow sparring with a partner, you need to focus on your opponent and not yourself, or you will get hit.

Heavy Bag Sparring

This is a great starting point for beginners wanting to practice their drills. Striking a heavy bag gives you an idea of what to expect when you come face to face with a real opponent. You get to understand how much force and speed you need to incorporate. It's a bag, so feel free to be brutal with your throw kicks, punches, elbows, and hand strikes. When the bag swings forward, use this to practice evasive tactics before striking again.

Dummy Sparring

This is also great for beginners who want to improve their defensive skills. Dummies are used a lot in martial arts and even in gun control because they are much safer. A dummy will be instrumental in learning offensive and defensive strikes and the use of both hands simultaneously. As with the bag, feel free to throw your strikes, but there is no need for evasion since the dummy cannot react. So, focus a lot on your power levels.

Circle Sparring

This is quite advanced, but even if you are a beginner, you will still have to face this at some point. The main focus of this drill is to learn awareness of your environment. In circle sparring, you are surrounded by six or more people who attack you one by one. Circle Sparring tests your speed, power, skills, and ability to react intuitively under pressure. There is no time to think. You either act fast or lose. Ordinarily, your fellow combatants are at the same skill level as you. But when your skills grow, circle sparring can become more intense because you will have more than one person attacking you at once. As a beginner, you might need to save this for last and understand other drills sufficiently first before taking on attacks from six people.

Additional Things to Note

Speed is of monumental importance in Taekwondo. Currently, how fast are you? How fast do you think you can be going forward? Sparring matches are very short, and they usually don't last for more than two minutes. Improving your kicks is an excellent way to improve your speed, plan your next move even before executing a strike, and plan for more than one kick in your attacks. When you have adequate preparation, you do not need to be outlining your next move while on the mat mentally. It should be done before you even step up on the mat.

- Faster kicks come from relaxed muscles, and this is why meditation and stretching are important. Tight, tense muscles will always react slower, never faster. Before practicing your kicks, relax your muscles so that your kicks come in a fluid, easy motion.

- Power is also of colossal importance in Taekwondo sparring. You must consistently hone your strength. Keeping this in mind maximizes the impact of your kicks or punches, and you can time your kicks or punches so that it collides with your opponent rushing at you. It multiplies the power of your attack and the counters speed of your opponent. To increase your power, you should also learn to incorporate squats and jumps in your warm-up exercises as they; build up thigh muscles. Remember to be cautious and careful with exercises and to perform them in the presence of a professional. Too much of these exercises might cause too much pressure that inevitably leads to injuries.

- One final thing to always have in mind is to be accurate with your kicks, strikes, or punches. One way of improving accuracy is to practice kicking small objects until you consistently hit your targets accurately. You will mostly find this challenging as they are smaller than what you are used to in usual target areas. Small targets don't only help you improve accuracy; they also help you to train your reaction towards a moving object. This training is vital because your opponent is a moving object in the ring, and you'll be skilled enough to direct your response with speed. Training with friends is also a good way to improve accuracy. Just ensure you're both outfitted in protective clothing.

Conclusively, Taekwondo is not the easiest sport or martial art. It will test your physical and mental capacity in numerous ways. Some will fly sky high, and others who crash and burn. As a beginner, you need to figure out what side you want to be on. Study the habits of the high performers in this art, and you'll find that they don't joke with their stretches, nor do they slack on their drills. They are also powerful combinations of accuracy, speed, and power. Strive to be the perfect embodiment of these things, and you are set for astronomical success.

Chapter 13: The Taekwondo Habit: Training, Discipline, and Mindset

Learning Taekwondo has several benefits. It is one of the most beneficial martial art forms to learn, as it improves your ability to defend yourself, and this sport also impacts various aspects of your life. Taekwondo improves your health, fitness, and mindset, and you will experience an overall boost in your quality of life by participating in this sport.

The many benefits of this sport stem from the diversity of technique and the discipline and mindset required to reach mastery. More than just a physical exercise or competitive sport, Taekwondo is a lifestyle that can empower an individual in various ways. People who engage in this sport can expect to gain a certain level of confidence and excitement in their life.

What Can One Learn from Taekwondo?

A good number of people take up Taekwondo classes for self-defense or to gain physical strength and agility. However, as time passes and you continue to train, you will realize that the benefits of Taekwondo transcend its physicality. You might not know this yet, but mastering the way of feet and hands can help you change your view of life and improve yourself in various ways. Some of the additional benefits of Taekwondo include:

Courtesy and Respect

If there's anything you'll learn from your very first Taekwondo lesson, it is that you have to bow to everyone and anyone. This act is not only done by beginner students, but even teachers and seniors take a bow in Taekwondo before proceeding with any action. One simple explanation for this is that it teaches respect.

By bowing before anyone regardless of their age, rank, or skill level, you learn courtesy, scaling down on your ego as well. You cannot bring your real-life status with you everywhere. Taekwondo also involves you bowing before an opponent. While this may seem ridiculous, this act packs in an important lesson; in real life, you must learn to show respect to people even if you have differing opinions or simply disagree.

Perseverance

There's a reason why perseverance and indomitable spirit are among the tenets of Taekwondo. It takes years to attain mastery of the art. You will practice continuously for weeks and months to move from one level to the other, building an attitude of perseverance towards your work. Even when you get to the highest point and earn your black belt, learning in Taekwondo can still be a sustained and sustainable aspect of your lifestyle.

This teaches you to invest in your tears and sweat to become a better version of yourself. That's how it is in the real world. Adversity will come your way, but you must stay strong and persevere if you are to harvest the fruits of your labor.

You Will Learn Something New Every Day

In Taekwondo, you will realize that learning never ends. No matter how much you have learned or the belt colors you've achieved, you have to learn new skills and develop yourself continually. The best martial artist is one who never closes the door on an opportunity to learn something new.

Discipline above All Else

As you begin your Taekwondo training, always keep in mind that discipline is vital to your success in Taekwondo and your daily life. Many things will try to push you off your chosen path. At some stage during your training, it might seem like you're not progressing as much as you should. In moments like these, it is up to you to decide how you want to respond going forward.

Taekwondo Training

By now, you probably know that Taekwondo is highly physically demanding. You will need a lot of physical power, stamina, and flexibility if you want to perform at higher levels. It is why Taekwondo training is best suited for the young and agile, but age is just a number, and anything is possible for anyone with enough willpower regardless of age.

Being young and strong is not enough to excel in Taekwondo, and many young people still have trouble keeping up with the pace of training. You will have to push yourself to the limits to build the right attitude and habit required to become a successful Taekwondo warrior.

Compared to many other forms of martial arts, Taekwondo is quite aggressive, but it has a very low injury rate or chance of permanent or serious injury. However, it is still important that you're aware of the dangers and rigor of what you're getting into. Taking up martial arts is more dangerous than painting or any other soft hobby. Therefore, you must take into consideration important safety tips and follow training instructions to reduce the chances of injury. The misconception that Taekwondo is a safe sport isn't the only one out there.

Getting Started? We Have News for You

There are two, actually. There's good news, and there's bad news. Let's just dump both on you right away and leave you with it. We'll start with the bad.

Taekwondo is hard; never begin with the illusion that you're going into a soft sport that is easy to master. As you will discover when you start your journey, going from white belt to black belt requires a high level of dedication and consistency from you.

The good news is that it is possible to fast-track your mastery and achieve impressive results. First, congratulations. The fact that you have read this book up to this point and have not stepped on the training mat is great. To celebrate this feat, you get a white belt, which is more than if you didn't step onto the mat at all. So, go ahead and give yourself a pat on the back.

Know that the decision to take up Taekwondo lessons means you have committed to do something challenging but amazing. But, as you will soon figure out, the journey from here to the top is an uphill climb. It is possible to feel lost at the onset, and you might even feel silly as you mess around trying to imitate moves of others who seem to move around gracefully with their fancy footwork and elaborate spin kicks.

So, how can you make Taekwondo easier for you to learn and fast-track your training? (Note - easier, and not easy. Taekwondo isn't easy, but you can make it easier by following a few simple tips). Keep the following things in mind as you begin your training and develop the proper habits.

Relax

If there's anything you need to know, it's that tense muscles don't work well in martial arts. Your moves will be slower, and your kicks and punches will be weaker if you're tensed up. You will also lose steam quickly during your training.

So, loosen up and relax. You will need to if you want to develop the right techniques. Practice how to relax not only your limbs but also your mind. Meditation and mindfulness practices are essential for this aspect. Practice regularly with a clear and relaxed mind, and you will see significant improvement in your technique. The more you do this, the more automatic and fluid your moves will become. You may have to actively will yourself to relax at the onset, but with time, you will find you don't have to think so much about it anymore.

Practice Regularly

You must attend classes and pay attention to your lessons. However, you will achieve remarkable results with more practice, meaning you need more time than the regular classes you spend with your instructors. You have to practice at home on your own. People who practice Taekwondo on their own at home are likely to do better than those who don't.

Your training should include solitary sessions to develop your form and build your technique at your own pace. Still, sparring is an important part of Taekwondo training as well. Research has shown that practicing under conditions you're likely to use as a motor skill will improve your mastery significantly. It is particularly essential if you're learning Taekwondo for self-defense or competitive purposes. It is important to note that as a beginner, you will be allowed to spar right away, but as you get a few levels higher, it will be an integral part of your training routine.

Exercise

Regular exercises are important for strengthening your muscles and improving flexibility. You need to focus on stretches and other routines that help improve the strength of targeted muscle groups.

It is recommended that you do stretch routines after your daily training (not before). Stretching out at the end of your workout helps keep your muscles from becoming tight and boosts flexibility. Your muscles are already warm and elastic after a workout, and you will achieve better results with your stretches.

You should also do routines that strengthen your core and hammies (hamstrings, hips, and glutes). You will be doing a lot of kicking in Taekwondo, and the effectiveness of your kicks depends on the strength of your core and posterior chain. Workouts like crunches, squats, and jackknives are quite beneficial for this muscle group. Also, include pushups, pullups, and other routines that strengthen your upper body for better punches.

Meditate and Visualize

Sometimes the most beneficial workouts are those you do without moving a muscle. With meditation and visualization routines, you can improve your skills and sharpen your mind while you're at work, cooking, or even in bed.

A lot has been said about meditation techniques in chapter four of this book. Go over it again if you need a refresher. Visualization involves you picturing yourself going through the motions of techniques to perfect them. It's like practice but in your mind. Research has shown that the same area of your brain that is involved in physically performing those moves is stimulated when you visualize yourself doing them. It helps build strong neural pathways to improve your skills.

These non-physical skills will also come in handy when you're too busy, injured, or too sick to practice physically and you have to be out of action for a while.

Conclusion

Taekwondo is one of the easiest forms of martial arts to learn, but that does not mean it is simple and rosy through and through. It takes determination and perseverance to go through the various levels of the sport and excel.

There is a wide variety of techniques and styles to master. You may notice that there are many variations in what you have read in this book to what you will find elsewhere. Many of Taekwondo's techniques have been developed by different masters. The sport is also globally governed by various organizations that adopt different rules and conventions. While you will find the lessons you have learned in this book instructive and beneficial, we implore you to listen to your instructors. Not only do they have the final say on the techniques you must master, but your instructor will also determine the pace at which you should learn them. You need to do what your instructor tells you if you want to get the best results.

Don't get ahead of yourself. Focus on mastering the basics and gradually work your way up. The spin hook might look fancy and sexy, but you must resist it until you are mentally and physically ready. The advanced moves and techniques will come later, and many are simply variations of the basics you are already learning. If you don't get the basics right, you are likely to struggle in the advanced stages.

Lastly, we hope this book was of benefit and that it will effectively supplement your training journey.

Here's another book by Clint Sharp that you might like

CLINT SHARP

Sambo

AN ESSENTIAL GUIDE TO A MARTIAL
ART SIMILAR TO JUDO, JIU-JITSU, AND
WRESTLING ALONG WITH ITS THROWS, GRAPPLING
STYLES, HOLDS, AND SUBMISSION TECHNIQUES

References

14 Basic Taekwondo Kicks (Everyone Should Know!). (2019a, November 29). Wu-Yi Taekwondo. https://www.wuyi-taekwondo.com/taekwondo-kicks

14 Basic Taekwondo Kicks (Everyone Should Know!). (2019b, November 29). Wu-Yi Taekwondo. https://www.wuyi-taekwondo.com/taekwondo-kicks

Basic Moves That Every Student of Taekwondo Should Know. (2010, February 15). Sports Aspire. https://sportsaspire.com/taekwondo-moves

billysmma. (2017, January 4). Basic Taekwondo Stances Explained. Legends MMA. https://legendsmma.net/basic-taekwondo-stances-explained

Blocking (막기 makgi) | Taekwondo Preschool. (n.d.). Taekwondopreschool.com. https://taekwondopreschool.com/blocks.html

Habits of a Taekwondo Martial Artist | Visual.ly. (n.d.). Visual.ly. Retrieved from https://visual.ly/community/Infographics/sports/habits-taekwondo-martial-artist

Josh. (2015, January 16). The 14 Basic Movements of Taekwondo. Martial Methodology. https://martialmethodology.wordpress.com/2015/01/16/the-14-basic-movements-of-taekwondo

Josh. (2017, January 16). How to Get Good at Taekwondo FAST(er). Martial Methodology. https://martialmethodology.wordpress.com/2017/01/15/how-to-get-good-at-taekwondo-fast

List of Taekwondo Kicks (Beginner & Advanced). (n.d.). Black Belt Wiki.

https://blackbeltwiki.com/taekwondo-kicks

Murphy, M. F. (2013, February 5). A Beginner's Guide to Taekwondo. Frank Murphy's Masterclass. http://frankmurphysmasterclass.com/2013/02/beginners-guide-taekwondo

Punches and Strikes in TaeKwondo: A Complete List | Tae Kwon Do Nation. (n.d.).

TaekwondoNation. https://www.taekwondonation.com/taekwondo-punches

Quality, F. (2016, December 5). A Brief History of Taekwondo. Fight Quality.

https://fightquality.com/2016/12/05/a-brief-history-of-taekwondo

Robert. (n.d.). Is Taekwondo Dangerous? Here Is What You Need To Know! Retrieved from

https://wayofmartialarts.com/is-taekwondo-dangerous

aekwondo Belt | Dos Taekwondo - Best Taekwondo Academy. (2017, September 26).

Dostaekwondo. https://dostaekwondo.com/taekwondo-belt-order-meaning

Taekwondo Belt System | Brisbane Martial Arts. (2009, August 20). Brisbanemartialarts.com.au. https://brisbanemartialarts.com.au/belts-and-stripes

Taekwondo Gradings – JUST KEEP KICKING. (n.d.). Justkeepkicking. Retrieved from http://justkeepkicking.com/taekwondo-gradings

Taekwondo Moves: Powerful Skills and Techniques to Challenge You. (n.d.). Made4Fighters. https://made4fighters.com/blog/taekwondo-moves

Taekwondo Punches & Strikes - Taekwondo Animals.com. (2018). Taekwondo Animals.com. https://taekwondoanimals.com/taekwondo-punches-strikes

The Philosophies Related To Taekwondo. (2017, January 25). Hong Ik Martial Arts. https://hongikmartialarts.com/philosophies-related-taekwondo

Tips for Taekwondo Students. (n.d.). Taekwondo Wiki. Retrieved from https://taekwondo.fandom.com/wiki/Tips_for_Taekwondo_Students

Walking Stance (앞서기 ap-sogi) | Stance (서기 sogi) | Taekwondo Preschool. (n.d.). Taekwondopreschool.com. Retrieved from https://taekwondopreschool.com/tutorialstance2.html

What is Taekwondo? A definition and short history - Master Chong's Tae Kwon Do. (2017). Master Chong's Tae Kwon Do. https://buffalotkd.com/what-is-tae-kwon-do

What You Need To Know Before You Start Taking Taekwondo.... (n.d.). Www.streetdirectory.com. Retrieved from https://www.streetdirectory.com/etoday/-wwjuuw.html

Printed in Great Britain
by Amazon